WHERE'S THE *ME* IN MUSEUM

Going to Museums with Children

Milde Waterfall
Sarah Grusin

Illustrated by Marcia Leddy

VANDAMERE PRESS
a division of AB Associates

Published by
Vandamere Press
A Division of AB Associates
P.O. Box 5243
Arlington, Virginia
22205

Copyright 1989 by Vandamere Press
Printing History
Second Printing August 1991
ISBN 0-918339-08-1

Library of Congress Cataloging-in-Publication Data

```
Waterfall, Milde, 1949-
  Where's the me in museum.

  1. Museums--Educational aspects.  2. Education of
children.  3. Children and adults.  I. Grusin,
Sara, 1951-     . II. Title.
AM7.W38   1988            069.1'5               88-1719(
ISBN 0-918339-08-1
```

Manufactured in the United States of America. This book is set in Janson.
Typography by Chronicle Type & Design, Washington, D.C.

Dedication

This book is dedicated to a world filled with the spirit of curiosity and the energy of discovery. For making that world familiar to us we are thankful for the children who inspired us, especially Josh, Ned, Claire, and Ben; two ever-patient husbands; the trust we have in each other; and the emotional and professional support of our friends.

ACKNOWLEDGEMENTS

We would like to pay special tribute to those people who were willing to advise and direct us as this book struggled its way into print: Dr. John Fines, Patty Pearson, Marianne Latall, Wende Walsh, Bill Blackwell, Barbara Matteo, Pat Berger, Ed Lee, Eddie Goldstein, Barbara Waters, and George Tressel. We owe a debt of gratitude to the Corcoran Gallery of Art as the first art gallery where many of the book's themes were discovered and where we met each other. Washington Focus, a non-profit organization, nurtured the idea by offering the first class, "Where's the Me in Museum" and made it possible to test the ideas in many museums with interested families. *Museum & Arts Washington* offered encouragement and provided opportunities to find people interested in museums. Finally, Barcroft Books in Annandale, Virginia introduced us to Art Brown, our publisher, who can re-count the many changes and revisions that have led to this document which he believed would evolve.

Table of Contents

Chapter One
Curiosity
Transcends

"Maybe children—maybe all of us, need museums most in order to learn to marvel or not to forget to marvel. Because we marvel at these wondrous objects . . . we eventually marvel at man, at what we are."

—Bruno Bettleheim[1]

While our children yearn to journey to every corner of the galaxy, many worlds on our own blue planet await discovery. Museums beckon to present-day explorers as an "other world" that can be explored without a rocket or supplemental oxygen supply. In museums, inquiring minds from the entire universe can meet, observe, and marvel at this world.

Where's the Me in Museum is an exploration and charting of the diverse and challenging world of museums when in the company of children. Traditionally, museums have commanded a certain reverence that has hindered both children and adults from enjoying the museum adventure. However, when museums are viewed as centers for exploration and discovery, a child's enthusiasm for the museum knows no boundaries. Museums offer families more than a checklist of things to see. They provide the opportunity to view those untouchable, revered "other worlds" as part of their own world. In an effort to encourage the family to participate in such an adventure, this book identifies what makes the family museum experience unique, how the presence of a child affects a museum visit, and what activities and attitudes nurture a love for museum-going.

---

[1]B. Bettleheim, "Children, Curiosity, and Museums," *Museum Education Anthology.* Museum Education Roundtable, 1984, p.18.

Where's the Me . . .

Museums preserve tangible evidence of life on this planet. Every museum-goer, small or tall, young or old, can be assured there will be something familiar in this seemingly uncharted territory. When a museum-goer recognizes part of himself in the museum, he has found a *Me*. There are *Me's* inside paintings and *Me's* riding rhinos. There are *Me's* who hide between the lines of the Declaration of Independence and *Me's* who keep dreams alive while hanging from a ceiling.

A museum-goer who is aware of all the different kinds of *Me's* found at the museum looks in every corner of the museum-universe for clues. There is a *Thinking Me*. This one makes decisions, formulates questions, and makes predictions. The *Feeling Me* responds with delight, anger, or concern to a Calder mobile or a box turtle. The *Building Me* creates, takes apart, and reassembles the world to gain some understanding of how it works. Then, there is the *Pack-Rat Me* who saves, collects, and classifies possessions to record and organize the disorder of the world.

When a five-year-old peers at a Degas painting, she searches for a *Me* that makes sense to her. A five-year-old may not know dance, or Impressionism, or how to pronounce Degas' name; but even a five-year-old has a *Feeling Me* who yearns to belong to the grace and beauty of Degas' world.

What difference does finding the *Me* make to the average child or adult museum-goer? The finding of a *Me* insures that the museum becomes a place to be comfortable exploring the mysteries of the world. The *Me* in the painting, or the beehive, or the First Ladies' gowns makes connections from the museum-goer to the museum world. A child who feels a connection with the world, who sees his or her *Me* reflected in the world, regards the world with more care and interest. Children who value artifacts and creations of their culture grow into adults who create and preserve culture for the next generation.

In the upcoming chapters, many *Me's* will surface in surprising and unusual places. What becomes clear to a family of museum-goers is that finding the *Me's* at a museum starts by exercising the habit of thought. A family who adopts the habit of thinking at the museum finds that the Degas painting, the stuffed bird, or the boots of a Civil War general can spontaneously generate many sorts of *Me's*. A family of thinkers can approach the museum's collection with the anticipation of rediscovering themselves in the world.

When an adult chooses to be at a child's side in a museum, the majority of the *Me's* that will be found will belong to the child. The adult shares in the discovery of the child's *Me's* by remaining curious about what the child thinks and by being willing to listen to the child. This book introduces some techniques and resources that have helped many adults and children bridge the long distance between their lives and the new territory of the museum.

Discovering the child's *Me* in the many objects that are encountered at the museum empowers the family. This empowering does not imply that through regular visits to an art museum, a child can identify four out of five Impressionist painters. Neither does a visit to a history museum turn a six-year-old into a walking encyclopedia, nor a science museum transform a mild-mannered toddler into a nuclear physicist. Rather, it is the exposure to new viewpoints on the world through art, history, and science that makes the museum-goer more aware of the scope of his heritage.

The term family in this book includes children who sightsee with favorite aunts, uncles, and family friends as well as the nuclear family. Indeed, the only way to define a family visit is to say it must consist of at least one big person and one little person who enjoy each other's company. The words, child and children, refer in a general sense to all age groups, not just those under five years. Because children vary tremendously in their abilities and skills, ages are defined only in special instances.

Just as family museum-goers come in every shape and size, museums reflect the same diversity. From the Smithsonian's megamuseums along the Mall in Washington, DC, to rustic farms and lavish historic homes, each museum is distinguished by its collections, its architecture, and the programs that it sponsors. What all museums have in common, however, is their dedication to preserving a part of man's heritage.

While this book is designed as a guide to help families enjoy museums, there is no "must-see" list of museums nor a recipe for a perfect museum visit. Subsequent chapters discuss the basics of child-adult museum-going, examine five types of museums, and provide resources that can enhance the museum experience.

Museum-going With Children

A museum visit in the company of a child contrasts with one taken alone or with other adults; however, some aspects are common to both adults and children. Although adults may act and express themselves differently from children, a child is just as able to think, feel, form opinions, and make judgments as any adult in the family.

During a museum visit, what distinguishes adult museum-goers from young museum-goers is the quantity of the adult's experiences. Adults are storage vaults of experiences. These experiences color the way adults perceive how the world works and create a feeling of confidence about what is true and correct. A child is less sure of how the world works. This lack of certainty is likely to bring a fresh viewpoint to the museum visit that an adult is not able to bring.

Adults who enjoy going to the art museum and who have gone many times alone or with other adults often forget what a spectrum of experiences art museums offer. In their rush to see a new and highly recommended exhibit, many adults skip over some very exciting parts of the museum. Outside the Corcoran Gallery of Art, two huge bronze lions and two enormous studded doors greet every visitor. Paradoxically, it takes someone with an unedited perspective to rekindle an awareness of the lions' awesome beauty and the grandness of the doors. A child's ability to renew an adult's sense of awe is one of the true wonders of the world.

The Museum-Goer's Bill of Rights and Responsibilities

Every museum-goer is embodied with certain inalienable rights. These rights are held to be true and, if so honored, will preserve the union of adult and child within the museum.

Each museum-goer is entitled to his interests and disinterests. *The Museum-Goer's Bill of Rights and Responsibilities* can be a liberating document for people who are beginning to trust the worth of their own feelings, intuitions, and abilities. Armed with the knowledge that they are not expected to like every work of art or understand every scientific invention on exhibit, the museum-goer can view the museum as a safe retreat that encourages freedom of thought and expression.

Curiosity Transcends

The curiosities that blossom within a family beg to be given room to grow. "How does it work?" "What is that for?" "Why did that happen?" are common questions in family life. In both children and adults,

---

The Museum-Goer's Bill of Rights and Responsibilities

- We have the right to our curiosity and therefore are able to identify our own treasures.
- We have the right not to like a museum or an exhibit.
- We have the right to be confused by what we find in museums.
- We have the right to be bored if there is nothing that seems interesting.
- We have the right to take the time we need to look and think while in a museum.
- We have the right to freedom of expression at the museum whether it is talking or being silent, or asking questions and giving answers.
- We have the right to be physically comfortable.
- We have the right to want to go home.
- We accept the responsibility for not damaging the museum or its collection.
- We accept the responsibility for listening to other opinions besides our own.
- We accept the responsibility for our own behavior.

---

curiosity transcends the expectations which contain "should have," "supposed to," and "just because." Curiosity transcends the fear of not knowing. It transcends the ordinary demands of family life.

The family museum visit allows a child to linger over the puzzles that his curiosity finds. Museum-going with an adult presents the child with the opportunity to be interested in whatever he or she chooses instead of staying with a group as in the case of a school field trip. Adults who are willing to keep their own concerns behind a child's and not rush the visit will cultivate a fellow companion to muse on life's puzzles.

Natural Curiosity and Cultivated Curiosity

Children have a natural curiosity about topics that have a direct impact on their lives. Bugs and animals have a natural magnetism. Dinosaurs have engaged interest ever since they became extinct. Roaring rockets and spooky caves excite children of all ages.

How can curiosity be cultivated when objects do not have the charm or enticing allure of a looming Tyrannosaurus skeleton or a piece of the moon? For children under the age of eight, paintings can be more aloof, and historical documents behind glass cases have even less appeal. How does an adult help a child find a reason to look at something like a landscape painting? Adults can begin by searching the object for something a child can recognize. They may find a *Comparing Me* in the gentle rolling countryside depicted in a 19th-century landscape and a familiar walking trail. In finding their *Me*, children must graft something from their experience onto the painting. Some families might enjoy finding their *Me* by imagining a bike ride along the path in the painting or an afternoon of skating on the small pond in the corner of a landscape.

Once the family finds something familiar within the work of art, a fuller exploration of the painting can begin. The act of finding this part of the family's familiar life in an unfamiliar painting allows the family to feel good about what they know and inspires them to want to know more. When families take a deeper look into the puzzles of art, history, and science, a well of curiosity naturally bubbles up.

Cultivating curiosity is often as rewarding to an adult as it is to a child. The secret to cultivating curiosity is knowing where a child's natural interests lie. Most children are concerned about basic issues such as their own vulnerability, their dependence, their ownership of things, and the amount of power they have in a relationship. They are also interested in fairness and justice. Recognizing these kinds of interests, an adult can apply the four tools of cultivating curiosity and almost always reap a harvest. The four tools are:

- A clearly presented dilemma.
- Language using terms children understand.
- A realistic goal considering the time and space.
- A worthwhile reason to look from the child's point of view.

Any dilemma or puzzle presented to a child needs to include all four of the above elements to be intriguing. The child's delight at having a puzzle or a problem to solve in some cases leads him to look more deeply within the surface of the object or work of art. To witness how curiosity can be cultivated, imagine a parent and five-year-old who are exploring the Corcoran Gallery of Art in Washington, DC. A large 18th-century landscape, Albert Bierstadt's *Mount Corcoran*, causes the adult and child to pause. Unfortunately, the average child under six possesses about seven seconds' worth of interest when looking at most landscape paintings.

In helping his child take a closer look, the adult suggests an imaginary adventure in looking. Capitalizing on the *Owner Me*, the "that's mine" perspective that resides in every five-year-old, the adult says, "Suppose that I gave you all this land in the painting, where would you put a cabin?"

The dilemma was clear and presented in terms a child could understand. The time to puzzle about a reasonable goal was provided since neither the adult nor the child was in a hurry. The realistic goal for the child was seen in looking for a cabin site in the painting. Cabins appeal to the *Pioneer Me* in everyone.

In the process of cultivating curiosity, the child feels important. He has gone beyond simply being the receiver of information about the painting to becoming a decision-maker. In the child's mind, he has entered the painting equipped with a more logical reason than a technical discussion of Bierstadt's use of light. Using his own thinking abilities, the child has focused on the painting carefully. He has noticed the mountains and the steep shadows, the angle of the sun, and the lay of the land. He has then been able to decide whether the view of the mountains is more desirable from the front or from the side.

The point of placing children in a *Mount Corcoran*-type of situation is that children are rarely presented with an occasion where they are the ones in a position of power. During their daily life, children are constantly the receivers of information and direction, food and shelter, gifts and love. Consequently, children beg to give, share, and choose for themselves and for others. Adults who are sensitive to this fact can offer the museum experience as one where the child can actively direct what is observed, thought, and felt.

A child knows choosing the sight of a cabin is a game of pretend. Most choices a child makes during childhood are actually "pretend" choices. Because the world of play is held together by "pretend" choices, this is not a new experience for a child. However, the value of setting up these choices and allowing them to occur may be new for the adult. By becoming familiar with some of the strategies that encourage a child to enjoy making "just pretend" choices, an adult learns how to create that kind of open environment where a family's curiosity transcends any physical or behavior problems.

The Chain of Expectations

Museum-going is an activity draped with expectations. Usually adults have selected a museum based on a friend's recommendations, newspaper or magazine reviews, or past experiences. It is possible that the adult has already formulated an opinion regarding what is going to happen. The National Portrait Gallery in Washington, DC, mounted an exhibit about Davy Crockett. The excitement over the possibility of seeing "real" coonskin caps infected one mother and her four- and six-year-old boys. With the help of home videos, visions of Walt Disney's Fess Parker danced in their heads.

Unfortunately, expectations overrode reality in this case. There, in a small room on the second floor, was the exhibit. It clearly explained that Davy Crockett, never, repeat never, wore a coonskin cap. His hat, visible in several small lithographs, looked more like a weather-beaten cowboy hat.

After years of daydreams inspired by Fess Parker, the mother was awash with disappointment. The children, however, were not troubled by the lost legend of the cap and eagerly bounced from the hat display to the display where "Betsy," Davy's rifle, was featured.

The first reason the children were not upset was that they did not share the weight of the mother's expectations. The second reason was that the dozens of other interesting artifacts, pictures of Davy's house, and accounts of a horse riding escapade offered the children a different set of Davy Crockett stories. The children grasped the authenticity of the objects and found their *Frontiersmen Me*'s even though the unexpected information had initially soured the exhibit for the mother.

As illustrated by the Davy Crockett exhibit, expectations must be kept in perspective during a museum visit. An adult may be disappointed by the discrepancy between what he or she expected to be there and what really is, but a child does not have as many of those expectations. Adults who openly accept the museum's portrait of Davy Crockett find it easier to help the child find worth in whatever it is he sees.

Classic Expectation No. 1: The Data Base

Going in search of facts or data to acquire is a classic expectation that many adults share. This acquisition of facts, however, has a limiting effect on the museum visit. Most children either drift into their own daydreams or escalate their poor behavior after ten minutes of being told facts.

A computer can house the complete *Encyclopedia Britannica*, but until a human being commands the keyboard, the information cannot be transformed into anything other than fact. Children are the transformers of their own time. It is important to introduce them to the facts, but it is just as important to allow them to determine how much or how little they can absorb.

Classic Expectation No. 2: What's Wrong With Us?

Newspapers and magazines regularly comment on museum exhibits. It is quite natural to take someone's word about what is worthwhile. Yet, this type of expectation has a subtle quality of keeping up with the Joneses that is tricky to recognize. Be advised: When an exhibit touted as wonderful has children looking for an exit, take a physical reading of the room. In the case of an art exhibit, check the work out from a child's perspective. Most paintings are lit for someone who is five-feet-two to five-feet-ten. Anyone who is taller or shorter has to compensate. The room may also be too crowded for the child to enjoy the art or may require reading plaques or long descriptions that are of no interest to the average four-year-old.

When children do not live up to adults' expectations regarding a certain museum exhibit, there can be disastrous consequences. Instead of trusting the child's reaction, an outsider's opinion—the reviewer's or the mother's best friend—is given priority. It is better for the family to forget about the experiences and reactions of others. No one needs to go to museums under duress. The time to reflect or compare what the adult felt about a painting is after the visit. Keeping score during the visit only creates pressure on the family to react to the exhibit just like the Jones family.

Classic Expectation No. 3: Adult as Limited Being

Wanting to be the authority puts pressure on an adult. In an effort to answer a child's questions, many adults try to present confusing, half-remembered theories from high school. Adults do not need to pretend to understand why electricity makes hair stand up. At the museum the answers to questions are readily available to adults and children. The family can turn to the exhibit or the staff when they need help solving problems.

Museums acknowledge that children retain what their parents tell them far longer than information they get from any other source. Interestingly enough, this is the case even if parental information is not accurate. Many exhibits are designed to give parents basic information quickly and clearly to help them answer children's questions. If graphs or other written material do not give enough information, a parent who says, "I don't know; let's find out," is cultivating the *Researcher Me* in both parent and child.

Children may know answers that adults do not know. When children are encouraged to share their expertise, they become more confident and enthusiastic about museum-going. The chapter on natural history, discusses questions and answers that may give adults some ideas on how to enlist the child's help.

Parent as Advocate

Families are important. With regard to museum visits, children are influenced just by the fact that they are there in a special place with their family. In one study it was found that, "Sixty percent of regular visitors to art museums attributed their interest to the fact that someone in their family took them to an art museum when they were children." [2]

Sometimes children see an adult as an adversary, as someone who makes sure that chores are performed, homework completed, and good behavior enforced. Museums offer adults a chance to be an advocate, a friend, and a helper. Becoming the advocate means that the adult is helping create opportunities.

At Rose Hill Manor Children's Museum in Frederick, Maryland, one child spotted a yoke that was used to carry two water buckets 100 years ago. He said to his adult companion quietly, "I wonder how heavy that is?" The adult politely asked the guide if it was possible to take the yoke off the wall and give the child a chance to feel the yoke on his shoulders. The guide honored the request because she could see that both the adult and child were responsible, careful museum-goers. The boy felt the rough wood and how heavy it was without two full buckets of water. Everyone talked about how difficult it must have been to walk and balance two buckets, the need to stoop over, and the

[2]Ibid.

subsequent aching back. Water must have been precious, the boy concluded. Clearly, the fact that the adult acted as a responsible advocate opened an opportunity for an experience not present on a regular tour. The adult helped tailor-make the visit for the *Working Me* with which all children can identify.

Opportunities constantly are passed by at the museum because many parents feel rushed or they do not want to bother anyone. Contrary to this perception, most well-trained museum tour guides, often referred to as docents, are happy to diverge from their routine speeches. Parents need to be aware of this willingness and encourage their children to ask questions. They also need to be ready to step in and ask the question themselves when they see an opportunity slipping away.

There are a few simple ways to encourage docents to deviate from prepackaged scripts. Try asking if the docent knows or can share any little secrets which he is unable to tell under normal circumstances. When a child sees that a docent is not a walking tape recorder, his perception of the docent's role changes from one where information is repeated over and over to one where someone has an inside track and can divulge all sorts of unexpected information. Another source of guidance at the museum is the guard. Many guards know a great deal about the paintings, artifacts, or exhibits. A guard also has an immediate and real knowledge of areas of interest in the museum. Rather than keeping the guard in the age-old role of disciplinarian, visitors can add to their visit by engaging the guard in conversation. However, guards and museum rules vary widely. Some guards are instructed not to talk. Some guards may not want to talk. In general, however, more visitors have benefited from asking a question of a guard than by letting the opportunity pass.

Building relationships with guards and docents serves another purpose in that it makes the museum more personal. A docent or guide who has shared personal opinion is less a stranger who has memorized facts and more a friend who has shared understanding and curiosity in museums. Some children have been known to ask for a return visit to a museum with the sole purpose of visiting the docent or guard. Many adults take for granted the opportunity to speak and meet with other people. Children do not. Connections with people, especially for young children, are often stronger than connections with places or things.

Where's The Museum in Me?

Families go to a museum for many reasons, sometimes to get out of the house on a rainy day, but more often because they recognize the museum offers them chances to get acquainted with a world that often remains hidden behind office, school, and home routines.

A museum is a place that collects, displays, and shares its treasures. The museum can offer ideas of why things are important according to experts in the field, but it is up to museum-goers to find meaning in these objects. In this book, the *Me* in the museum is found only by those families who enjoy cultivating their curiosity along with the objective of having a good time.

This chapter has given the family as museum-goers some understanding of the fundamentals of visiting museums. Since museums are part of the real world, Chapter Two examines some of the practical and physical aspects of children inside museums. Chapters Three through Seven identify the unique qualities of different kinds of museums, the possible trouble spots, and the survival skills necessary to have a good time.

This book encourages the family to enjoy museums to the fullest. It is important that adult museum-goers realize that they are in a position to create a love for museums within children. Adults can offer the gift of museum-going to this new generation. Not only are there many *Me*'s waiting to be found at the museum, there also is the *Museum Me* who is awakening in every family. Childhood and adulthood are full of experiences that are treasured and catalogued in our memories. Museums treasure and catalog the memories of many, many families and creatures who inhabit this world. When the family sees in the museum a reflection of what they are, life as most families have known it in the museum may never be the same.

Chapter Two

Museum Visits: The Basics

S andy is on the edge of her seat and has been for the past 20 minutes. Alex is bored and thirteen. Johnny is feverish and four-and-a-half. Their mother has reluctantly taken up peace negotiations and, as for father, he has been anxiously looking for a place to park for 45 minutes.

Can any museum rescue this discouraged crew? This chapter offers some solutions to Sandy, Alex, and their parents' problems. Unfortunately, Johnny's need falls clearly in the area of modern medicine and no museum can drive a fever away.

Museum visits require energy, but families do not always realize how their energies are conserved and expended. Certain elements of museum visits tax a family's energy reserve. This chapter offers insights into some of the logistics of a museum visit; it also encourages the museum-goer to recognize different styles of learning and how they can affect the visit.

The Four "B's"

While there are no guarantees or recipes for success when it comes to museum-going, every adult museum-goer needs to become familiar with the Four "B's" before entering a museum. These "B's" are not related to the buzzing-around variety; nevertheless, they can sting a museum visit right in the foot if they are neglected. The Four "B's" of family museum-going are Behavior, the Building, the Break, and Bathrooms.

Behavior

Many people think that children naturally understand the difference between public and private behavior. The truth is that very few children can make this distinction. Home is a place where children can run, jump, and scream with delight. The rules at home are often very

different from the rules that apply in public places like museums which are shared with other people.

Although this book advocates the individuality of thought expressed in the *Museum-Goer's Bill of Rights and Responsibilities*, children and adults must realize that poor behavior is not a right at the museum. By calling on their own skills of observation, children can be helped to understand the different rules without being told about them. "I wonder why no one is touching the paintings," is a subtle way to say, "Don't touch!" Other clues to public behavior can be noticed in the same way. "Do you see other people jumping or shouting? Does this look like a gymnasium?"

Many parents worry about how their child might behave during a museum visit. Prior to arriving at the museum, it is a good idea for parents and children to discuss how visitors act at the museum. Talking about public behavior accomplishes three things. First, it clears the air regarding what appears to be allowed and what is not. Second, it creates a reference point, such as, "Remember when we talked about this." Third, the children can begin to assume the responsibility for their own behavior. Over focusing on behavior, however, can prevent many adult and young museum-goers from enjoying the museum. If adults can find a way to make children aware of what is expected of them at the museum without using threats and bribes, then they are able to turn the family's energies to the enjoyment of the museum. When the family's energies remain locked in a war of wills, the visit's potential for sharing has already collapsed.

On the other hand, poor behavior at the museum may have a physical cause. Two hours later when a fever surfaces or a stomachache starts, it is suddenly understandable why the child was acting up. By asking a few simple questions about the child's physical health, parents can offer a way for the child to explain why he is not behaving well.

Sometimes when poor behavior starts, it only signifies a cry for attention. Perhaps the child is unable to find something of interest at an exhibit. When this difficulty occurs, an adult can try to redirect the child's interest. In this way it is easy to discover if, in fact, the child is unwell or is just looking for something else.

The range of acceptable museum behavior differs widely according to the type of museum. While hands-on museums and children's museums are free from "no-touch" rules, there are many rules of sharing and respecting the museum's property that must still be obeyed. Art museums present the most difficult behavior problems for families because many adults have a fairly rigid idea of how art should be enjoyed. In reality, there are very few rules outside the "no-touch" or "no-climb-on" rules. It is permissible to sit down on the floor in front of a painting provided that the traffic flow of visitors is not blocked. Sitting on the floor is not comfortable for everyone; parents should note that when children sit on the floor, it may be the only way they can get a good look at a painting. Museums often shine lights on paintings that render the painting unviewable from a child's standing height.

Behavior is also influenced by a child's age. Children from ages three to five will have a hard time adjusting to a world of not touching. Discussions about public behavior are helpful but not always successful; however, using the authority of the museum guard can take the wind out of a disobedient four-year-old. Although children might pretend not to understand the no-touching rule, they do understand their uneasy feeling when approached by a uniformed authority. Some chil-

MY CHILD-AWORKOFART
ANONYMOUS
DATE UNKNOWN

dren benefit from comments like, "Look how important this art is. There are all these guards around to protect it."

The Building

An often overlooked part of a museum visit is the museum building. Although it is a commonplace experience for adults to enter large buildings, children, especially first-timers, are intensely aware how different it is from home. While adults are equally affected by the uniqueness of the museum building, they consider the tall ceilings, heavy ornate doors, and mountain of steps as unworthy of the family's attention. Naturally, a child is bewildered when he is dragged up the stairs, pushed through the doors, and ushered through the lobby of a place that appears hugely different and intriguing.

Feeling secure in the museum's space is imperative to everyone's successful museum-going. A seven-year-old who knows the territory of the museum feels important and confident and is ready to have a good time. If a child has unanswered questions about the building, his mind will fix on his concerns and jeopardize any possibility of his enjoying an exhibit.

Another way families experience buildings is by moving about inside them. Open spaces beckon. The curving, grand staircases promote fantasy and the constantly moving escalators seem mysterious and inviting. To even the most casual observer, it is obvious that children react strongly to the qualities of their surroundings. By taking time during the first part of the visit to guarantee the child's security, the family can proceed with their visit assured that they now know where they are and what the building looks like.

Noticing the building also serves the wider purpose of letting children know where they are. Take time to ask a small child to name five ways in which the museum differs from his home. Look for the skeleton of the building—the pillars which hold it up, the curious shapes of ceilings, the source of natural or artificial light. If several building features are pointed out, the museum building becomes more familiar and less threatening to the child. Do not let the museum entrance remain "just a door." Instead, consider the door what it truly is, a beginning.

The Break

Food and drink are never far from a child's thoughts. During a museum visit, the best way to cope with these thoughts is to incorporate the break into the museum visit routine. Since energy is at a premium during museum visits, the break needs to be used as an energy replenisher, not an energy drain. Families can engineer a variety of ways to take time out for themselves within their museum visits, but many families have found that the bag lunch is the most adaptable form of refreshment.

One reason the bag lunch method gets preferred status in this book is that, no matter how cosmopolitan the child, cafeteria and vendor food rarely tastes how he assumes it is going to taste and, consequently, often goes uneaten. With a bag lunch, the family knows what lunch will be. They know they have what they need. They know about how long it will take. Equipped with these knowns, a family can turn its attention to reflecting about what they have seen, what they still want to see, or simply to passing the potato chips.

While it is fairly easy to find places that are suitable for family dining in familiar locations, finding a place to buy a meal at a new museum may be a source of anxiety. Families with young children often find it easier to plan on bringing their own food. If nourishment is suddenly needed at 10:30 a.m. and the cafeteria does not open for another hour, the family is prepared to satisfy this need on their own.

During summer, spring, and fall, the family can enjoy a brief venture to the museum grounds or a nearby park for a break. Another

alternative retreat for the family who has driven to the museum is a quiet moment in the car. When bad weather or cold temperatures prevent going outdoors, special permission can be obtained from the guards to bring bag lunches inside and consume them in the cafeteria.

Taking time out from the museum is important to every family visit although not every visit requires a bag lunch or a cafeteria date. Some families have tremendous staying power and are able to keep doing the museum hour after hour with just a few sips at the water fountain and a granola bar. Sitting down to read a story, walking around the museum gardens, or chasing the birds on the lawn are all ways to renew a family's energy. Regardless of the type of break taken by the family, they should try to use these few moments for reflection and relaxation.

Bathrooms

Before any museum visit gets started in earnest, it is important to locate the bathroom. Since the bathrooms are not always centrally located, it is a good idea to know where they are and at what distance. Bathroom emergencies are unnecessary if families make a point of using the facilities before they enter an exhibit. Children who are required to wait almost always end up having to make a last-minute dash. This can be disastrous, especially if there are lines of people waiting to use the bathroom.

Families can easily combine the activity of noticing the building and finding the bathroom. At the Corcoran Gallery of Art, children find the bathroom captivating because of the unusual furnishings. When visiting older museum buildings, families may find many of the original bathroom fixtures intact or, as in the case of the West Building of the National Gallery of Art, the walls are black Missouri limestone that are full of fossils. This presents another opportunity for the family to use this "B" to notice what is different about this museum.

In summary, the Four "B's" form the basics for family museum-going. By dealing with possible behavior problems, noticing the building, planning a break, and visiting the bathroom, many potential problems can be easily avoided. The family can then turn their attention to sharing experiences and enjoying the total museum visit.

Four Museum-going Styles

Sensitivity to museum-going styles is a keystone to a successful family museum visit. Watch two children with different museum-going styles enter the National Museum of Natural History. One immediately races around the giant elephant stopping briefly to try two or three different earphones; another walks quietly up to the earphone, listens intently for four or five minutes, and gazes at the elephant.

How children and adults understand what they see and read at the museum varies widely. Consequently, the museum visit is bound to be affected directly by the museum-going styles of the family. One of the things children love about museum visits is that museums allow them to learn about things the way they want to learn. The important thing to recognize is that a child who moves quickly from item to item is not necessarily bored. Many children have a hard time making sense of anything unless they can touch it. Parents need to be aware of four basic museum-going styles. They are the Researcher, the Hit and Run Champ, the Button-Pusher, and the Dreamer. The Researcher generally enjoys details, taking in exhibits as they come, content to add to his body of knowledge in the order in which the museum has presented the information. By contrast, the Hit and Run Champ, equally as interested in detail, likes to see the entire exhibit before selecting which part to examine. He may zigzag from one exhibit to another to compare and contrast information. He is definitely not predictable in his approach. The Button-Pusher is the child who loves to touch and manipulate, learning through other senses than sight. Finally, the child who immediately imagines the people in the wagon train or what it would feel like to be an astronaut, the budding philosopher and idea man of the future is the Dreamer. Obviously, there are many variations of these four, but getting acquainted with them and recognizing some of the characteristics can enhance the family's museum visit.

Museum visits by family members with different styles can be potentially disastrous. If the Researcher is in the company of the Hit-and-Run Champ, then the museum visit could be a logistical nightmare. The Champ will need to conquer the territory first and the Researcher will yearn to take his time and settle in.

The ability to focus on one subject is unpredictable with preschoolers up to third graders. Adults who recognize this fact have fewer behavior problems in public because they do not place unreasonable demands on the child's attention span.

Young children are generally the most experimental in their museum-going styles. Preschoolers lie down on the floor of the art gallery and zigzag from one wall to the other; they insist on looking at the same painting over and over. Young minds gain confidence from repetition. When a painting or a turtle shell appeals to a child, adults should honor this interest and return to the item until his curiosity is satisfied.

When three or four children are involved in a museum visit, logistics become challenging. Adults cannot please everyone all at once in the same place. Sometimes it helps if the family can separate occasionally to allow each child a chance to enjoy the museum at his own pace. This presupposes that there are at least two adults or a responsible teenager counted among the group. On the other hand, learning to tolerate contrasting museum-going styles helps children accept the needs of others. If this is not practical, making separate visits, using babysitters, or bringing extra adults are all ways families can apply their awareness of different museum-going styles to their visit.

Museums have become more and more sensitive to the varying needs of visitors and offer a wide range of activities to suit different styles and interests. Look for each museum's potential for fulfilling these needs. Call ahead or check with the information desk for live demonstrations, discovery rooms, films, and special tours.

Parents need to remember what Frank Oppenheimer, founder of the Exploratorium in San Francisco, said: "No one flunks a museum." There is no test at the end of the visit. Educators are often denied the time, space, and materials to address differing styles or methods of learning. Families who recognize style differences can celebrate rather than discourage them. When an adult's museum-going style conflicts with a child's, negotiations can be tried between a child of at least six years of age and an adult. Under normal circumstances children enjoy most things their parents show interest in. Indulging in a special art exhibit or marveling at the craftsmanship of primitive tools, however, may require adults to plan museum visits on their own. Adults who want to encourage museum-going in children may find they need to shelve their own interests temporarily.

That *Age-Old* Question

Many parents of very young children wonder when it is appropriate to begin taking them to a museum. Unfortunately, there is no simple answer. Children vary widely in their interest, and in their capacity to focus on, and become involved in, a painting or an exhibit. Parents who are aware of their child's abilities and interests will benefit from thinking about why they want to take the child to a particular museum.

A good reason to go has made many difficult visits successful. In Chapter Six a family's dedication to the success of a museum visit shows that interest is a key factor when taking children to museums.

When deciding whether a child is ready to go to a certain kind of museum, adults must remember that their enthusiasm can be very infectious. What gives an adult pleasure can give children pleasure, but parents should be advised not to expect a child of four years to conceptualize the way an adult does. The adult's interest can spark the child's interest, but the child's stage of development may prevent him from sustaining a long look.

A child's developmental stage does affect how and what he or she experiences. For example, children ages four and under have a very physical understanding of their world. They take in information every minute, but that information is not in the form gained from reading or listening for long periods of time. Activity and lots of touching and talking are realistic methods for four-year-olds to learn.

Certain kinds of museum activities seem to beckon to various age groups. Four-year-olds make great story-tellers. They love to hear stories and they love to make them up. Mystery and intrigue continue to fascinate five- and six-year-olds, especially when they are offered a chance to do some real detective work at the museum. By seven or eight years, children are beginning to have some sense of historical time and enjoy figuring out the puzzles of history, such as events that sparked the Civil War.

Age is not an accurate indicator of interests. For example, some three-year-olds can be fascinated by an exhibit of Wyeth paintings. Let curiosity, not age, determine the selection of the exhibit and the length of time that may be needed.

From the Adult's Perspective

The adult on a museum visit needs to play the roles of audience and backstage manager at the same time. The adult needs to be an attentive listener and observer of the child's reactions and interests and of his interactions with the museum. Simply by being willing to listen, adults show how they value the time shared with their children at the museum.

Each of the following chapters addresses issues unique to those museums. In general, as noted in Chapter One, parents need to accept that the child is clearly the one who holds power during a museum visit. It is his museum-going style that sets the pace and his curiosity that needs to be cultivated. What to see, where to go, how fast to go, and in what order are all decisions children need to make during their visit if they are to feel truly in charge.

If dinosaurs can sustain a child's appetite for 90 minutes, then there is no real reason for the adult to object. When adults nudge children away from their interests, they are in effect taking control of the visit originally meant to be for the child.

Arranging a museum visit to honor a child's interest does not mean that adults need to be timid about participating. In fact, one role that adults can take is that of offering choices. Some children need verbal prompts when their interest begins to wane. "Would you like to look out the window?" "Should we go to the next room? Should we go downstairs?" These types of choices gently and encouragingly direct the children to look elsewhere.

The extent of preparation before a museum visit is highly individual. Beyond knowing the choices a specific location has to offer, there is very little actual preparation required to have a successful museum visit. It may make an adult feel more secure to understand the meaning of Post-Impressionism, how electricity works, or when man walked on the moon; but, to a young child, these facts are not always relevant.

Reality Descends

Some people say a parent's sense of timing is innate. This may be so, but anxiety, sticky fingers, and a whiney voice can transform even the best of parents into a beast. The time of day for the museum visit is very critical. A parent full of good intentions is one thing, but taking a child accustomed to afternoon naps to an art museum at 2:00 p.m. endangers the mental and physical health of the whole family.

The practical side of timing museum visits is acknowledging that most children are at their best in the morning when they are well-rested. Planning a visit that starts when the museum opens its doors is a good idea. Some children who are truly afternoon children, however, can proceed directly to the museum after lunch. In fact, many museums, especially the ones popular with schoolchildren, are far less crowded in the afternoon when all the school tours have retreated. Sometimes evening visits, as offered by many major museums in Washington, DC, and elsewhere, combine the atmosphere of a bedtime story and a museum visit. Weekends, of course, are difficult because of crowds. Most of the time, however, a family can avoid crowds by choosing to visit something besides a very popular exhibit.

When visiting a museum for the first time, it is a good idea to research what the museum has to offer in terms of parking, refreshments, and hours of operation. Many museums are closed on certain weekdays and holidays and their sources of food may also have limited hours of availability. Parking at most metropolitan museums is almost always difficult. The alternative to driving is using public transportation. Generally, public transportation is a treat in itself for children and it allows parents to enjoy talking before arriving at the museum. If public transportation is not available it is a good idea to arrive early to park, possibly in a paid lot. Bringing a stroller allows young children to rest during the family's walk to and from the museum and thereby conserves their energy for the museum visit itself.

During the time in the museum, parents should remain alert to the signs of museum visit fatigue. A child who sings choruses of, "Can we go home now?" or "Are we going to leave soon?" is giving a clear sign that he is worn out. The physical needs of a child deserve respect. A few questions can reveal if the child is simply bored, tired, or not feeling well. Assessing a child's condition takes only a moment, but ignoring clear signs of fatigue can bring a museum visit to an abrupt and unpleasant end.

You've Got to Know the Territory

The basics of museum-going are actually very few. Knowing the territory, that is, the realities of the museum visit and the abilities of the child, ensures a museum visit's success. This chapter has given the museum-goers different aspects to consider when planning a museum visit with a child. Wherever the family goes, the basics outlined in this chapter create a foundation for enjoyable and educational visits to the museum.

Beyond the logistics of museum-going, families need to become comfortable with themselves and the museum environment. Museum-going is most successful when a family has considered ages, abilities, energy levels, and transportation. It is very difficult to find meaning in an exhibit when Sandy fidgets, Alex yawns, and Dad is worried about the parking meter. Take the time during the next museum visit to review how the family follows the the Four "B's." Chances are the more "B's" that are included in the visit, the more *Me*'s will be found.

Chapter Three
Art Museums: The Seeing Place

"Having eyes but not seeing beauty;
having ears but not hearing music;
having minds but not perceiving truth;
having hearts that are never moved and
therefore never set on fire.
These are things to fear."

—Sosaku Kobayashi
(indirect quote from Kuroyanagi, T., *Totto-Chan.*)

Taking a child to an art museum begins an adventure that never ends. Being together as adult and child at a place like an art museum is a union in search of meaning in the world. This is not an everyday family activity, yet it is a type of adventure that never fails to bring special insights into a family's everyday life. It is the simple fact of being together and choosing to take time to appreciate art together that inspires those first steps into the adventure of art.

Visits to an art museum perform another function besides providing a means of being together. Because they are "seeing places," art museums enhance the way the viewer sees the world. Learning to appreciate art does not mean that an eight-year-old can pronounce correctly all the Impressionists' names or even recognize who created what. Rather, family art appreciation means a recognition of the visual influences in a family's world. Art inspires a heightened awareness of the patterns and colors that are a part of everyday life and this recognition changes the family's perception of the world.

If parents have not seen the need to take their child to an art museum in the past, it may be helpful to notice how our culture honors and affirms other endeavours. Stadiums are built because sports are highly valued. Research laboratories exist because of the importance of sci-

ence to our society. In the same way, art museums exist because contemporary culture recognizes the worthiness of art in modern life.
Denying this experience to a child keeps him from a part of his culture
and the knowledge that our culture honors, protects, and fosters art.

For many families art museums remain a mystery. This chapter offers families several ways of looking at art so that the mystery is not
quite so big. In the last part of the chapter, games and activities are
suggested to help families become more comfortable looking at art. Because adults have many behavioral expectations about art museums,
the section "From the Adult's Perspective" examines how to deal with
specific behavioral and logistical problems. When the mystery is gone,
the family can begin to enjoy art and their exploration of the world
together.

What's So Great About Art?

Throughout civilization art has been the tool that hammers out
meaning in the world, paints the day with grace, and frames a culture's
beliefs. Art is the evidence of how civilizations have envisioned their
world. From hunting scenes in caves to depictions of religious and sec-
ular ceremonies, art has meant survival. Many cultures have depended
on their art to find a herd of antelope or give them a record of a historical or seasonal event.

Art has the power to open windows on the world. When two 19th-
century American artists, Albert Bierstadt and Thomas Moran, painted the wilderness, their paintings so moved politicians who had never
been west that they began to recognize the importance of preserving
the land from development. Those paintings were very influential in
the politicians' decision to create a National Parks system. Through
their paintings, sculptures, and drawings, artists bring to light new
aspects of the visual world that surrounds us. Some people doubt if
they truly saw a sunset before they saw a Turner sunset or recognized
the intricacy of a sunflower before they saw Van Gogh's.

For the Young at Art

Families who are young at art are individuals who are not familiar
with art. The whole subject of art is new to them. The terms are
strange; at times they need a translator. The art museum itself is often
considered a foreign territory, a place where artists unknown to the
average family exhibit their works. The young at art have basic ques-

tions about art and art museums. If some of these questions are answered now, these new art adventurers can begin to enjoy the museum.

The first concept families need to understand is that art is a made thing. Art does not just happen. In this vein art represents an act of creation in the same way a hot air balloon or a steam locomotive represents an act of creation. When families view art at the museum, they are carrying on the tradition of appreciating a creative effort.

Creating art is an act that requires the artist to make choices. Those choices limit the colors, shapes, concepts, and textures that appear in the work of art. Artists are similar to family members in this way because everyone in the family is an experienced choice-maker. The Calder mobile in the East Building of the National Gallery of Art is a collection of choices: red choices, black choices, and choices about the mobility of different shapes.

After just a few minutes at an art museum, visitors can easily see why the issue of choice is so important. Many an art curator has been stopped in his tracks by the inquiring child who wonders why some perfectly new statue does not have arms or legs. The answer is found in the simple fact that the artist *chose* to create it as it is.

This matter of choice clearly answers the ever-present, always-asked questions, "Why is this art?" and "What talent is required to throw paint on the wall?" The answer to these questions and many others which surface during a visit is the same. The reason an object is considered art has nothing to do with what it looks like. It is art simply because it was the artist's intention. He intended to create art and, therefore, the very act of creating the painting or sculpture means it is art. The artist or "do-er" creates the art; the viewer decides whether he or she likes or dislikes the work of art, not whether it is art.

The other obvious question that pursues the family in appreciating art is, "Why is this work in the museum?" The answer is again based on the idea of choices. The reason some art is found in museums is that people make choices based on their experiences in the field of art and see worth in some of it. Not only did the artist make his or her choices about how to make the art and the viewers decide whether they like the art, but also the museum representative had to choose to include the work in the museum's collection.

The next question that haunts, or rather tickles a family's art museum visit, is this: "Why are there so many naked people in the art museum?" For centuries the human figure has been considered beautiful and timeless. Many artists have chosen to leave off clothes because selecting a certain style of clothing classifies the figure as belonging only to a certain period of time. Also, the human figure is, in the words of an eight-year-old, "very hard to draw." It is quite natural for children to giggle and snicker at nude statues. In truth, some of the works make adults giggle too.

These kinds of questions are so basic to an art museum visit that there is a tendency to overlook them. Answering these questions honestly and completely allows children and the accompanying adults to clear away some of the misconceptions about art that can handicap a visit. A child who is so embarrassed by a sculpture that he cannot look at it without snickering benefits from simple observations of parts of the sculpture, such as the materials, the face, the hair, the hands and feet, the stomach and shoulders, until finally it no longer seems strange. Families who wonder together at the similarities between a sculpture of found objects and the collection of "stuff" under their basement stairs eventually puzzle about why the artist's collection is at the museum and their things are not. What has the artist made exactly?

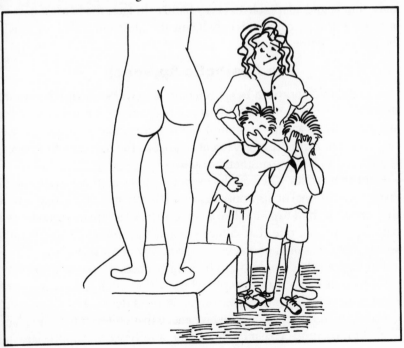

Why has someone determined this sculpture is worthy of a look and the collection under their basement stairs remains something to hide? The answers families find to these questions are not as important as the act of questioning and wondering together as a family. Children who are allowed to share their confusion in the world with their parents generally enjoy questioning and learning more than children who are afraid to question. Being young at art means a family is beginning to feel comfortable in the role of viewer. When they giggle or when they ask basic questions of themselves and the museum, they are interacting with art. These types of reactions are the foundation for all museum visits. When a family can build on it, the state of being young at art becomes a land of limitless adventure.

Four Approaches to Art

Art museums are seeing places, special places for the eyes. The four approaches to art described here help families in their looking and understanding. These approaches are exciting adventures and eye-opening exercises for the family. From the aesthetic to the storymaking, from the historical to the elements of art, these approaches are amazingly simple and adaptable to every family. In fact, the hardest part of beginning to appreciate art is convincing the adult and child how much they already know about it.

The Aesthetic Approach

An aesthetic approach to art refers to a viewer's initial response to the work of art, the uncensored natural reaction one has with a work of art. Since there are no minimum age requirements for museum visitors, anyone, from the effervescent toddler to the most aloof teenager, is qualified to have an aesthetic response.

Confusion arises when adults expect a child's aesthetic response to take a conventional or appropriate form. Parents are in for a long wait if they expect a child to sound like an art critic. An aesthetic response is a natural response, one that comes from within the child in his own words, not the words of an experienced critic or art historian.

Finding out that children can have an aesthetic response to art may come as a shock to many people whose vision of childhood is one of endless mess-making, toy-wrecking, and mass destruction. There are generations of museum-goers who believe that children have no place in an art museum and that children cannot fully see and appreciate the meaning in art. The truth is that children experience strong, open, and unmasked responses to art. They see with a sincerity and clarity that often eludes an adult.

No one denies that children feel something about a painting—good, bad, or indifferent. The language a child uses to express these reactions frequently differs from what a parent expects. The problem for adults is that in the garden of popular expressions, it is difficult to see the flower for all the weeds. It can be misleading, often embarrassing, when the child simply says, "I don't like it," or "I think it's dumb," or the articulate compliment, "Yea, it's neat."

At an exhibition of the early 20th-century American artist and illustrator, N.C. Wyeth, a three-year-old boy was drawn to *Blind Pew*, the pirate painting. "Yukky man, yukky socks, yukky shoes," the little boy began chanting. Three or four times during the morning visit the child returned to the "yukky" painting and rechanted his chorus of "yukky man." In his own terms the child was reacting to the painting. It may have frightened him, he may have hated the pirate in the painting, but his expression was a genuine, strong aesthetic response.

As children grow older, there is a corresponding growth in adult expectations regarding how older children should express themselves. If the adult is frustrated in the seven-year-old's inabiliity to go beyond, "Yea, it's neat," there can be several causes. First, check to see if the child can see the art. Poor lighting and paintings hung at an inappropriate height for children can account for a lot of the child's frustration. Second, a child's lack of art vocabulary can inhibit his response. Consider trying the Elements of Art approach described later in this chapter as a way to expand the whole family's art vocabulary. Third, when a child is not expressing himself, there may be something else troubling him. Look for physical explanations, such as symptoms of illness or an uncomfortable personal problem. Last, the child may just be having a negative reaction to a certain painting. There are many paintings at an art museum that may cause a child to feel uncomfortable or insecure.

Above all, parents need to avoid showing displeasure with any form of aesthetic response from their child. By shushing the child who giggles at a nude statue or frowning when a child rushes at a painting shouting loudly, "There's my dog," adults tell a child that his aesthetic responses cannot be trusted, that they are not what they should be. In reality, "Yea, it's neat," is a perfectly acceptable aesthetic response from viewers of any age.

While the actual words that make up an art vocabulary are one problem, the offering of personal interpretations in a public setting may be unfamiliar to many families. Some families may be uncomfortable expressing their actual feelings. There are many works of art that evoke unpleasant feelings like sadness or grief. For visitors who have difficulty sharing these highly personal feelings, it may be helpful to note a few phrases that help draw out the words. Try starting sentences with, "This painting reminds me of———," or, "When I look at this painting, I feel———."

Finally, the key to enjoying the aesthetic approach to art is the parent's readiness to accept his child's reactions. There can be no discrimination, no editing. Some parents readily admit they are not experts on the subtleties of "neat" or "yukky." Similarly, children cannot communicate the despair of human existence. Children need to learn to trust their aesthetic reactions; they cannot attain this trust if they sense parents are ready to disapprove their words.

Remember art museums are "seeing" places, not testing places. If nothing appeals to the family, there is nothing wrong with leaping forward centuries in time and going on to see another gallery. With the aesthetic approach, it is the sharing between parent and child that takes priority over acquiring art facts. The adult's most important role is to accept without censoring the child's response, whatever it is.

By following the conversation of a tour of several five-year-olds, the reader can begin to see how to discover an aesthetic response and how children can create bridges into a painting that an adult would never find by himself.

Robert Motherwell is a contemporary abstract painter who was the focus of a special exhibit at the Corcoran Gallery of Art. Many of his works display bold shapes on large canvases. For many viewers the initial response is confusion. There is a feeling that there is more behind the shapes, that this canvas means something, but what?

Standing in front of several children who were seated around a large Motherwell painting, the adult began by turning to the children and saying, "I think we need a detective." (By making this statement, the adult knew she would create excitement.) Following this statement, she asked, "Who knows what a detective does?" (This age group rallies quickly to answer seemingly simple questions. The question itself allows the child to feel he is capable of winning at this game.)

The children responded, "Detectives find things out, solve mysteries, fix problems."

"Well," she continued, "I spent a long time looking at Mr. Motherwell's painting and I think things are missing, but I'm not sure." (Here
she has given them a statement of truth and invited them to begin to
help solve the problem.)

"Do you think you could try to help me decide if things are really
missing in the painting?" (This was a clear invitation to try to help,
affirming the child's ability to help. The question was asked after lay-
ing careful groundwork and giving the children time to think and look
at the painting. Here the adult began to work out manageable rules for
the work to follow.)

"How will we know if something is really missing or if Mr. Motherwell just made it look that way?" (This question presented another
option for the children to explore. The painting was now open for their
ideas and clues.)

"Now, have a careful look," she said, "but remember in art museums
we only touch with our eyes. When you have a clue, come tell me."
(Immediately, the children felt secure enough to let their eyes go and

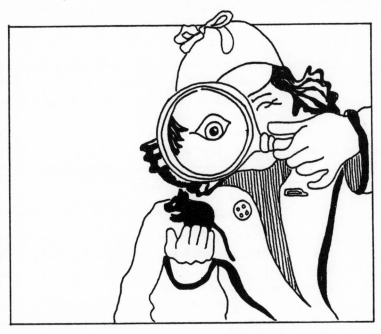

they began to discover great evidence. The adult was careful not to judge any statements.)

"Oh, yes. Something really was here. Look at the scotch tape; it's fuzzy," said one little boy.

"I see the glue," responded another child.

"Yes, the paint stops here and here," one boy said while pointing to an outlined shape.

After several minutes of discovery, one five-year-old boy came up to the adult and said, "It's just like my daddy." (This child had made a connection to Motherwell's painting by seeing how it was made. It helped him understand some part of his world. It would have been easy for the adult to be sarcastic because the response was so far from her own personal experience or to ignore the clue. Instead, she beckoned.)

"Really?" the adult asked.

"Yea," the little boy said confidently, "my daddy was here and now he's gone."

"It's like my life," volunteered an adult who was watching the children. "There are trails of things that were once there and now are gone." (Other adults and children were able to make this connection. Their aesthetic response was based on looking at the small details.)

"It's like bits of memory," another adult concluded.

This example shows that an aesthetic response is a very worthy approach to art for adults and children. By carefully looking at this painting, a five-year-old child was able to experience and share a poignant and truly remarkable insight, but it took some very careful examination before the aesthetic response surfaced. Similarly, the family on a museum visit may find that the aesthetic response is not always immediately forthcoming. However, those viewers who choose to take the time to look deeper into the painting can be richly rewarded.

Storymaking

Making up a story about a work of art is a powerful and delightful way to approach art. Most paintings and sculptures, especially narrative landscapes or seascapes, provide excellent visual stimulation for a family to explore a work of art. Storymaking seems to be most popular with four-, five-, and six-year-olds, but almost everybody enjoys a good story. With children under four, stories need to be kept fairly brief to accommodate their short attention spans.

When a family turns to an artwork in a museum, the museum grants the family the time and opportunity to make a story, that is, to make it their own by imagining people, animals, and events inside the artwork. When children and adults find a mountain landscape, they realize they may never walk in that mountain wonderland, but making up a story about the landscape permits the family to find the *Me* in the painting. Entering a mountain landscape offers the *Backpacking Me* to make some decisions about adventure and safety. That same mountain landscape is filled with views for the *Naturalist Me* to consider the possibilities this land offers. This approach to art lets the viewer get into the work by asking him to look closely at the painting to find ingredients for a story.

Following is a description of how an adult begins a story about *Mount Corcoran* already referred to in Chapter One. Notice how the parent guides the story around elements within the painting, thereby enabling a careful look and a subsequent storytelling effect.

"A little girl lives over here behind the mountain with her mother and father," begins an experienced adult storymaker. As the adult points to a particular area of the painting, she continues, "Her parents have told her never to leave the yard." The mystery and excitement in the adult's voice intrigue the child. "But," the adult teases, "she leaves. And she comes around the side of the mountain just about here." A few gestures toward the painting focus the child's looking. Finally, the adult looks expectantly at the child and lets her voice begin to trail off, "And then right there she sees a little, tiny. . ."

With this type of opening, a child can leap into storymaking with the little girl in the painting, what she saw, and what was going to happen to her when her parents found out. Together the adult and child can look into the painting for clues about their story.

As a story evolves, it is important for the child to feel the same kind of acceptance from the adult as during the aesthetic response. If the child says, "And the little girl saw a ghostbuster," then the parent must accept what is said and build upon this idea. A child's logic can baffle adults. Meeting a character from a popular 20th-century movie along a 19th-century mountainside would certainly be an unlikely occurrence, but obviously not in this child's eyes. It is the adult's responsibility to nod in agreement and comment, "Yes, right, a ghostbuster, which is very unusual because a ghostbuster is someone we see in a movie." The

success of the storymaking approach rests on a child and an adult's ability to play together with their imaginations.

How a story begins often influences whether a child is able to construct a continuation of the story. The most successful way to make up a story is to pretend. Notice the difference in tone when a parent says, "Let's pretend someone has given us this land and has sent us this painting so we will know what we're getting," and, "What would it feel like to stand here?" Pretending clearly signals a departure from the present, whereas standing does not involve the storymaker with any activity. The best stories are ones that are highly personalized. To help a child in beginning a story, try what one expert storymaker does: Use several senses to create a real "you-are-there" atmosphere. "Suddenly, a twig snapped in the pine woods behind her," is much more inviting than, "She walked by the pine trees." Likewise, "It's probably cold over there," does not intrigue a beginning storymaker like, "The old woman who lived in the forest was sick and out of firewood on a very cold January morning. Her dog left the cabin in search of help when he smelled the scent of . . . "

Storymaking at its best allows the art viewer to enter an imaginary world with ease. The first spoken suggestions get the viewer into the work directly. Many a grandfather has tucked in his grandchildren on Christmas Eve with a suggestion about Santa Claus. Which one works better? "Shhhhh, did you hear any footsteps on the roof?" or, "Now children, if you listen later tonight you may hear sleigh bells." The former suggestion is powerful and unlocks the imagination within seconds. The latter is condescending and has only one "if" to give the imagination flight. The best kind of story opening needs to have a direct "you-are-there" quality.

An adult's willingness to participate affects the story. If the adult's participation is limited to asking "what-happened-next" questions, then the story does not have an adult coauthor. Instead, the activity has become a form of interview.

Storymaking with art is a creative act in itself and builds an appreciation of the creative aspects of art. Storymaking encourages its participants to begin to read the work of art for clues as to where all the different types of *Me* can be found at the art museum.

The Elements of Art Approach

With many families, the most curious things about art are the physical and optical properties that affect art. For the young at art, the technical, almost scientific, side of a painting or sculpture offers an interesting and satisfying way to approach art. Understanding why certain colors mixed with other colors create a feeling of happiness or confusion enables the museum-goer to see what is going on inside the work of art.

For purposes of our discussion, the basic elements of art are color, line, shape, and texture. Artists are people who are experienced in knowing how these elements can be put to work to create a desired effect. During the first few visits to an art museum, the family may feel visually lost. In reality, however, a family probably knows more about the elements of art than they realize. Everyone can identify colors and recognize shapes. These activities are the basis of the elements of art approach—-that is, using the eye to find an interesting area and enjoying the new perspective. It may be helpful in this approach for the family to increase their art vocabulary. The ability to describe what they see in words allows a family to share their reactions. The follow-

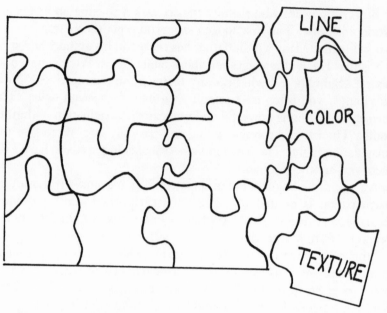

ing four sections include ideas on how to begin to see and then speak about the elements of art.

Color

Any member of the family can identify colors and compare their lightness or darkness and how they look in the company of other colors. With a few clues, however, the looking can go beyond the simple identification to the effect of the color on the viewer.

Color is probably the most obvious art element. It can influence one's feeling of the work and is often what is remembered most. Some of the properties of color are intensity, brightness, and contrast. When a color is very intense, it is very strong, such as fire engine red or golden sunset yellow. The duller the color, the softer it appears, such as the filtered brown-grey shadows of the forest or the muted blues of a cloudy seascape.

The brightness of color refers to how close a color is to light or dark. The darker the colors, the more they resemble black. The juxtaposition of dark and light and of dull and bright colors defines the contrast within art. The reason the shark's eyes have a strange gleaming cast in *Watson and the Shark* (National Gallery of Art-West Building) is that the shark's body is a dull grey and the water is a murky green-grey in contrast to a vivid yellow for the eyes. Colors that are opposites, red and green, purple and yellow, orange and blue, have a tendency to vibrate when they are placed next to one another.

The study of color is fascinating. There are physical reasons why colors have become associated with certain objects in our culture. The red or yellow of a fire engine signals visual alarms. Signs advertising ice are often an icy cool blue. An artist takes advantage of all these technical properties of color and of viewers' emotional attachments to make choices about colors and their appropriate use.

Observations about the colors in the painting can draw in the child's interest. "This grass looks green, but it's not the same green as these trees. I see three shades of green. Do you think there are more?" "The color of your shirt changes from blue while we're in this room to black when we're outside. I wonder why?" By talking about color in this way, the parent and child are personalizing their observations, finding a *Me* in the art museum. In the meantime, they are gaining additional vocabulary for sharing their thoughts.

Line

The element of line is a little more subtle than color but equally important. Many artworks have fairly obvious lines. Other works, such as sculptures or abstract works, use the shape of an object as the line. As with color, the properties of line affect the viewer's feelings about a painting. Curvy, gentle lines seem to flow off the painting while very straight lines give a feeling of precision and exactness.

The thickness or thinness of a line, like the intensity of a color, tells the viewer how important the element of line is. A skinny, very narrow line does not have half the power of a broad two-inch-wide line. The direction of the line is also very important. Horizontal, vertical, or diagonal lines create a sense of balance or imbalance. Some artists, like Gene Davis, have made paintings consisting entirely of vertical lines of color. Finally, the relationship of the lines to one another is noteworthy. Lines can be parallel, intersecting, or separate from one another. Lines can create pathways for the eyes to travel, focusing or highlighting areas for the eye.

Many educators suggest that children pretend there is no color in the painting, just the lines or outlines. Sometimes children can focus on one element if they are allowed to edit out the strong element of color. By peeling away the colors, the artist's use of line becomes more dramatic. Once they talk of lines, adults can help refine specific vocabulary. When an adult says, "That thick line running from side to side," the meaning is clear to the child. As adults see confidence growing in the children, words like "horizontal" or "vertical," when shared, become gifts, not instructions.

Shape

Shapes have four categories or choices: natural shapes (random and rarely straight), geometric shapes (circles, squares, rectangles), positive shapes (objects), and negative shapes (backgrounds). A painting with Goldilocks jumping from the second story demonstrates positive and negative shapes. Goldilocks is positive and the sky is negative.

Examples always help children know the territory. An adult can create words describing or capturing shape such as, "The sun looks like a circle." "How many squares do you see in that church?" Identifying shapes requires a visually disciplined approach. As with line, it is wise to help the child peel away colors in order to concentrate on shapes.

Texture

The texture of an object is defined by how it would feel to touch it. The artist has an infinite variety of textures from which to choose. Certain paintings by Van Gogh create objects that seem as though they could be plucked from the painting because the texture of the medium is very thick and the two-dimensional paintings takes on a three-dimensional quality. Henry Moore's sculptures beckon to be stroked because their surfaces are so infinitely smooth. Some 17th-century Dutch still-life artists painted satins so shiny that they appear to be real. Sensing whether the surface is rough or smooth, pebbly or gritty, contributes to the viewer's overall feeling about the object.

In an art museum, texture is experienced through the ability of our eyes to do the touching. Color, line, and shape can be navigated mentally in a way texture cannot. Awakening the child's sense of touch through an adult's observations can build a bridge between the painting and the child. The statement, "That velvet collar would feel so soft and smooth," invites the child to feel in his mind's eye. An adult who uses vocabulary that excites the senses, such as, "mushy," "gritty," and "smooth as steel," helps a child enjoy texture without having to touch it with his hands.

In summary, the elements of art offer adult and child a means to begin to notice all the different choices an artist makes during the creation of the work. In some ways, learning about these elements is like taking apart an old radio. Once all the pieces are on the table, it is possible to see what makes it work. Knowing some of the elements of art helps the family understand how art works. This brief discussion on the elements of art is meant as a beginning for the family. It shows that everyone is qualified to make observations about art. The statement, "That pink is the color of Lorraine's blouse," is just as valid an observation as, "The rose-colored vase recalls Victorian times."

Increasing one's visual literacy with this elements-of-art approach expands the family's sensitivities to these elements in everyday life. Colors, shapes, lines, and textures do not simply influence the perception of how art is made; these elements of art affect the viewer in very personal ways from the color and type of clothes they wear to the way they decorate their homes.

The Historical and Cultural Approach

The doors of history and culture offer another interesting approach to art. Inside every work of art, there are little treasure chests of history waiting to be discovered. By learning to read the painting or sculpture for its historical and cultural content, the adult and child can share a very rewarding exploration of art.

This approach is based on what can be learned directly from the painting, not on how much history the adult or child might know. This approach uses the clues right there in the art. Its success can be seen in fitting the historical clues to the experiences of the family.

The art museum often includes several historical facts about a work of art within its accompanying plaque. Dates are good reference points. If a painting was finished in 1936, then the viewer needs to find a way to refer to that date through something in the child or family's experience. For children from four to seven, personal history is the best solution. For example, "Was a member of the family born then? Is that the kind of hat Uncle Dick wore?" Children seven years of age and older are ready for a larger time scale. They can understand that their grandmother had her first baby in the 1930s and, when faced with a painting depicting the breadlines or hardships of the Depression, they might enjoy knowing how her life reflected these difficult times.

Geography also opens many doors into understanding art and the artist. "Where was the artist from?" "Is there something about the artist's country of birth which is relevant to the family?" "Did Grandpa go there in the war?" "Do you remember reading a story about Italy?"

"Did the third grade recently complete a study of Russia?" These questions penetrate the ideas a child already has and connects them with the
work of art. Making geographic references with works of art gives children a better idea of where they are in respect to the artwork and the
artist and fosters a *Worldly Me* who is thrilled to book passage on the
incredible journey within art.

The subject of the painting is also a historical reference point. "Is it a
landscape of Montana before it was settled by white people?" "Why are
the people dressed that way?" "Does the room look like your room?"
"What is different about it?" "Do you see a television?" "What did
these people do all day besides sit around?" "Does the painting depict a
famous war or an event in history?" Asking these kinds of questions
helps a child in two ways. First, he can focus on a particular aspect of
the work. Second, by looking for answers within the artwork, it becomes less intimidating. When a child begins to make sense of art in
this way, he will not fear art museums. Instead he will open their doors
with increasing confidence in his ability to enjoy art.

Opening doors into history and art is accomplished by creating these
types of personal reference points. It is a way of connecting with specific objects within the work, one which many adults find easier than
the aesthetic approach. A Cézanne still life might simply look like their
grandmother's old fruit bowl, but a still life with a dead bird or fish
might refer to a time when more people hunted and fished for their
food. The mere presence of some objects within a painting is historically significant. New technologies and evidence of political events and
social injustice are examples of the types of history that might be evident in a painting. A contemporary painting may have been produced
the year someone in the family graduated from high school or the year
Disneyland opened. These seemingly unrelated events are reference
points for the family, ones that help everyone to realize that many historical events occur concurrently. Further, it is important to realize
that even a five-year-old can make this type of historical connection
with a work of art.

Art produced in specific periods often gives deeper clues about the
people and their culture during that time. To modern eyes, ancient
cave paintings reveal the importance of survival in man's early history.
Some families may wonder what Gene Davis's stripes will tell other
generations about this era. Is it possible that some of the cave dwellers

were mystified by the one who kept drawing on the walls just as some of the present generation cannot figure out why an artist would choose to paint so many stripes?

While it is clear that history has many tales to tell through art, adults may try to turn this approach into a school-like lesson. The tendency for many adults is to share everything they know about the work, the artist, and the subject of the painting with the child; but, in fact, the child does not need to be told anything to appreciate it. Most of the history can be discovered together by sharing close observations of the work. Styles of clothes, hair, and architecture serve to date a work of art. Portraits offer viewers an excellent way to read history in art. Notice, for instance, the formal or informal setting and the items chosen to be included in a certain painting.

Museums give plenty of clues for families regarding the history of a particular artwork. As mentioned earlier, dates, names, even geography can offer families doors into history. Sometimes special paintings have extra clues. For instance, *Watson and the Shark* has a complete description of the actual events depicted in the painting inscribed on the frame. Often there are brochures available that can provide some insight into the history of the artist or the work itself.

The advantage of taking tours is that often the docent will reveal the story behind the painting or the artist. Guards will occasionally offer tips. During one visit to the National Portrait Gallery, a guard pointed out that in a certain Gilbert Stuart portrait, George Washington's eyes seem to follow the viewer wherever he or she stands.

The historical and cultural approach to art is a wonderful way for families to discover art. As the family notices scenes that are common to their everyday world—festivals, ceremonies, moments of sadness, happiness, or beauty—the world of art becomes more familiar and less confusing.

Finding the Right Way

Whether the family uses the four approaches described above or any number of other approaches to art, it is of primary importance to accept and enjoy their own abilities, interests, and understandings. Visitors go to art museums to see works of art, to view another person's interpretation of the world and maybe to find new meaning in their own understanding of the world.

In each family there will be times when children will be satisfied just looking at art and others when they hunger to make a connection to their own life. The approaches in this chapter provide the adult and child with different ways to appreciate art. There is no right or wrong way to view art; neither is there a right or wrong way to feel about it. Finding all the paintings with triangles is a worthy adventure. Deciding to count the shades of blue in a painting's sky is a first-rate visual exercise. Looking for textures in art that would make an eye-catching pair of socks can be downright rewarding.

During a visit to the museum the family has the opportunity to experiment with some of these approaches to art. Viewers should not be daunted by facts and theories they do not understand. Remember that all that is really required is the willingness to look together. Every museum-goer already knows enough to make the looking meaningful.

From the Adult's Perspective

For many adults an art museum visit is the supreme test of a child's behavior. These adults are constantly worried that the accompanying child will touch or harm valuable art objects or embarrass the family in some way with inappropriate behavior.

Addressing a child's need to touch is an adult's first job at the art museum. Even though many sculptures and paintings beckon to be touched, adults need to establish that an art museum is only a seeing place, not a touching place. Some children respond to the idea of touching only with the eyes.

Misbehavior during an art museum visit may be affected by whether the child has been allowed to set the itinerary. The two most unfortunate adult practices in the art museum are: (1) nudging the child along to the next painting or gallery when the child is clearly absorbed in what is before him and (2) holding the child back when it is clear nothing holds his or her interest. With either practice, it is the adult's itinerary being honored, not the child's. In Chapters One and Two, museum-visiting behaviors were examined more closely. Suffice it to say that it is essential to deal with these two issues, behavior and itinerary, to fully enjoy the museum visit.

Aside from the discussion on a child's behavior, it is worthwhile to say a few words about adult behavior at the art museum. Many adults are overfocused on the behavior of their children; they feel their children are on display in this public place, not the art. Children will be children at the art museum, not short adults. When an adult forgets his expectations and becomes comfortable with the child and his actions, everyone can begin to enjoy the museum visit. Children who know an adult is genuinely interested in what they see and think are less likely to misbehave because they are secure in knowing somebody cares about them and their thoughts.

Apart from these behavioral barriers to art museums, there are some physical reasons that may diminish the quality of the family's museum visit. A common problem is the lighting of the art. Many museums and galleries hang art too high for the average four-foot visitor to get a good perspective. In addition, the glare from spotlights can reduce a painting to one giant reflection, rendering it impossible to see. Adults who doubt this problem need only try getting down on their knees in front of a large painting, especially ones with heavy coats of varnish. It is immediately understandable why children do so much fidgeting while looking at the art; they are just trying to get a good look at it!

In the case of sculptures and small objects housed in cases, it is impossible for children to observe anything but the light reflected on the cases. It is no wonder that a child may find the case more interesting than the art inside it; it may be the only thing he or she can see well.

In combatting the physical barriers in museums, adults first need to observe how their children are looking at art. If the child moves or squirms around, the display of the art may be to blame. There are several solutions to this problem. Lifting the child allows him to see better, but this can be hard on the adult's back. Small children will benefit from a brief ride on an adult's shoulders if only to get an idea of what there is to see. Older children simply need to be given the chance to find a way to see the painting from the side or across the room. Another solution is to seek out those galleries that consciously mount the art at a child's height. For example, the National Portrait Gallery consistently hangs art in a lower position than many other galleries, thus making the art physically more accessible and easier to enjoy.

There is one more thought about appreciating art. Many adults and children share the misconception that art is easy to comprehend and, therefore, something must be wrong with them if they do not understand it. Nothing could be further from the truth. It may be comforting for all museum-goers to realize that art can be as intricate and complicated as Einstein's theory of relativity. Art is sometimes hard to understand; but just as most people cannot understand the theory of the universe at first glance, it is unrealistic to think that art can be understood in an instant. A large part of the adventure into art is the willingness of adult and child to see what they have never seen before, to think what they have never thought before, and, in simple terms, to know things they did not know before. An art museum is a seeing place, but as the museum-goer's understanding of art grows, it becomes more than just a seeing place. It becomes a place where there is a fitting together of ideas, history, and people, and a place where museum-goers can become familiar with their world.

Gallery Games

Gallery games present adults with a bag of tricks to interest children and themselves. Adults can use these games or combine them with ones invented for the occasion. One suggestion, however, is for adults to limit the number of games played during a visit. As with any activity, games can become tiring when played too often.

Postcard Games. Adults can pick up some postcards from the gift shop before the visit. Children enjoy hunting for the painting in the gallery. At home the child can select the ones he likes best and arrange them for a home exhibition.

Hide And Seek. Child and adult alternate hide and seek roles starting each game with, "I'm hiding in part of the painting. Try to guess where I am."

Shall We Save It? For landscapes, seascapes, and still lifes, museum-goers can imagine the painting without certain items. The adult can be the developer wanting to clear away all the trees or someone setting the table for a party. This type of looking recreates the painting and follows the artist through the choices that he has made.

Reading Faces. For portraits and paintings and sculptures with many people in them, adults can try this type of beginning: "I'm going to invite these three people to dinner. What do you suppose they like to eat?" Or, for some interesting insights into how children view their babysitters, try saying, "In this room is your next babysitter. Who do you think it should be?" This game helps the child to notice the faces and details about the person.

What Just Happened? Both adults and children can try to imagine what was happening within the artwork a few minutes before the artist captured it.

What Did You See? Both adult and child can study a painting for a few minutes, then look away. One person quizzes the other on what is actually there. "Is there any red? Where is the person looking? Is there a window?"

The Child as Artist (What the Doing Does)

An important aspect to any art museum experience is creating art. Children who have held a paintbrush, mixed endless colors, or faced an empty page approach a work of art with an understanding that comes only from doing. Giving a child the opportunity to create art actively engages their minds in a way that seeing art can never accomplish. The child's choice of an art medium is very important. Although one mother, a free spirit, vowed never to saddle her children with the confining lines of the coloring book, she found that when given a choice, one of her children adored coloring books, yearned for them, and relished coloring in the spaces. Adults can find many how-to-draw books on the market. Indeed, there are children who view these books as salvation, as a way of creating what dances in their heads but resists getting down on paper.

Creativity is being redefined daily. It is important when a child shows a genuine interest in any artistic activity for the adult to encourage this interest, knowing that the child's choices will flourish as he enjoys what he is doing. Also, by doing art, the child's capacity to appreciate the works of other artists is undeniably strengthened.

Post Visit Activities

Noticing the effects of art and design can be continued during the ride home and incorporated into daily family activity. The world offers infinite opportunities for the eye to distinguish shades of green in a clump of trees or textures within the home. The more observations that are made, the more one's eye begins to see the patterns in nature and in the family's life.

Other resources can be reviewed in the museum shop, local library, or bookstore. Families should not overlook the joy of postcards sold in the museums; these mementos can remind the child of what he saw. Some children may start a collection. Others just like to use them to tell someone else about their visit. At the end of this book there is a selected bibliography for families interested in expanding their knowledge of art.

The *Me* in the Art Museum

An art museum is a place that honors the great art of the world just as natural history museums pay homage to the many wonders of the earth. The art museum visit makes art accessible to the adult and child. By opening their eyes and minds to art, viewers find not only the *Me* in museums but also the meaning in works of art.

In this chapter several approaches to art have been presented to help the adult and child who are young at art make their visit more meaningful. Going to an art museum is an activity that encourages the family to notice and value the many landscapes and portraits that comprise everyday life. Most days pass all too quickly for the family to have a chance to get a good look at who and where they are. At the art museum the family has the time. By learning about the visual world at the museum, the family can begin to expand their knowledge of how art affects everyday life and how everyday life is reflected in art.

Chapter Four
Natural History: Wonders of the World

"Life is such a personal thing, wrapped up within the being of every living creature that it is sometimes hard to realize how intimately each life is connected with a great many other lives."

—John Storer, *The Web of Life*

N atural history is the story of the world. Making sense of the story requires the collection of thousands upon thousands of samples of the world from microscopic protozoa to rare red diamonds to mighty mammoth tusks. It is a story with intriguing twists of plot where major characters appear and disappear from the face of the earth. A natural history visit is a time when the world stands still for the family of man, woman, and child to reflect on the infinite variety and preciousness of life.

Samples of the natural world are unlike the art at an art museum which represents what someone thought or felt about the world. They are unlike the man-made artifacts found at a history museum which serve to record human events. The collections of natural history simply honor the natural world. These parts of the world, however rare or common, provide evidence that the world is truly wonder-full.

Where's the Natural *Me*?

All homo sapiens are thinking mammals. Big thinkers, little thinkers, logical and illogical thinkers all recognize that this unique capacity for thought sets homo sapiens apart from other forms of life. The adult and child can enjoy natural history together by using this natural ability. Natural history presents endless opportunities to be human, to think, and to discover.

With art there is the desire to interpret what has been created and what it means to the individual viewer. In a museum of natural history, vast collections of rocks and minerals, or of butterflies and moths cause the museum-goer to marvel at the existence of such diversity and splendor. While marvelling is a worthwhile response, many museum-goers sidestep the connection between personal experience and a case of rocks or dead butterflies. It is a rare viewer who is able to understand how stuffed birds or dinosaur skeletons can enrich their lives. This chapter seeks to find the *Natural Me* who inhabits the museum. Successful natural history museum-goers are a species of chameleon that are able to incorporate the objects and creatures on display into a pattern uniquely their own.

Types of Natural History

The pursuit of natural history can take a family to the four corners of the earth, on a journey into the center of town, or simply for a walk around the block. Wherever the family finds natural history, their experience will deal with two basic categories: living and non-living. The zoo, arboretum, and local nature center recreate living natural history as naturally as possible. The plants and animals are all alive in these settings, but the museum is a keeper of non-living things—stuffed animals, bones, and shells.

A wide variety of experiences can be enjoyed within these two categories. Megamuseums, like the Smithsonian's National Museum of Natural History, offer collections from millions of years of existence on this planet, organized into three floors of wonders. The advantage of such a large museum is that it offers something for everyone. Smaller museums of natural history, such as the Calvert Marine Museum in Solomons, Maryland, present excellent opportunities to focus on a few selected subjects in a more intimate and less overwhelming atmosphere.

At any of these locations, the purpose remains the same: to get close to nature. A family can be surrounded by nature in the course of daily life, but the nature found in the museum differs in that it is organized and often labeled or explained.

The impact of this difference can be illustrated by 500 butterflies suddenly lighting in the backyard and then taking flight. Any witness

:o such a phenomenon could only gasp at the gloriousness. In contrast, it the Naturalist Center of the National Museum of Natural History, 500 butterflies are arranged in colorful display, clearly identified, and available for endless hours of discussion and viewing.

Elements of Looking at Nature

While the last chapter discussed how ways of looking at art influenced the viewer's response, looking at natural history is defined not by *what* is seen and *how* it is seen but simply by the *opportunity* to see it. The factors that create this opportunity are time, location, and action.

Time is a tremendously important factor to consider, especially for a child. With natural history, time is not clock time—that is, how long children are allowed to wander around or when it is time to go. Rather, it is the novelty of stopping time, suspending nature's time in order to take a moment to look around. When a turtle scuttles across a path in the woods, this is live turtle-time. When a guide takes a turtle shell and allows a child to see inside, feel its surface, and test its weight, this is suspended time, a non-living turtle-time.

The next element of looking at natural history is how the location dictates what is seen and how it is absorbed. For instance, a nature center or wildlife refuge runs on nature's time. There is excitement in being there and being witness to this event. In contrast to the freedom of movement at a nature center, space is limited at a zoo. All the animals are in habitats created for maximum enjoyment. The opportunity to see animals that were once only seen in the wild should be cherished.

The last factor is action. At a nature center, the action is of primary importance. The animal is free to act on its own and it is only by chance that a visitor can observe it. At the zoo, beavers can be seen busily building a lodge. Few would ever see this in a natural setting. The zoo has an added advantage in that it does not place a viewer in any personal danger. At natural history museums, all three factors—time, location, and action—are frozen, thereby allowing the visitor to concentrate on what is there.

The above factors all affect how families react to natural history. Let three separate experiences with a red fox illustrate how important it is to recognize these differences. Suppose that during a walk down a trail on a beautiful day, a red fox darts across the path. It is a very exciting, ready-made wonder. The excitement of seeing an actual live fox thrills the observer. Although there are no cases, no classifications, and no explanations regarding the fox, its fleeting presence makes this natural history experience exciting.

Across the county a different family spots a red fox at the zoo. It is easy for them to get close to the fox and examine its coat. The fox's space has been limited and its official name posted by its cage. The family can see what the fox eats and not wonder if they are next. They can ask questions about foxes and marvel that foxes live among suburban sprawl. Limiting the fox's space has given the family time to watch him live in his environment and learn about him.

At a natural history museum, the stuffed fox stands in a glass case. His space *and* his time are limited. There is no danger, no action, no worry. The family walks by and Sally says, "Oh, look at the fox," and no one runs for cover. However, the label is there, perhaps his environment is there, and he is not going to run and hide or disappear inside his den. Gone are any entertaining aspects of natural history. In its place, however, are dozens of clues about life as a fox. It is a rare visitor who would recognize a fox track or know where to look for its home. Yet, all these clues are given by the natural history museum through its ability to freeze the world. It takes away the danger, it removes the visually mesmerizing live animal, and presents an opportunity to get close to the fox.

Mark That Question

Although questions can lead the eye when discovering art and will be used to lead the family in the other types of museums yet to be discussed, questions seem to occur spontaneously with natural history. Nowhere is it more apparent than with natural history, especially with natural history museums, how questions can increase the understanding of the world.

Questions are vitally important to the museum-goer because they indicate what is being thought and understood. Barbara Waters, Cape Cod Natural History Museum Director, believes that, "As long as children are asking questions, they are thinking, interacting with other people, finding sources of information gathering data—all the elements of problem-solving." Problem-solving is an important life skill because whatever a child becomes in life, he or she will certainly need to solve problems. Asking good questions is the first step in problem solving.

Notice how Waters asks a group of kindergartners to solve the prob-lem of a turtle shell with simple, but carefully chosen, questions.

BW: I wonder what happened to the animal that lived in this shell?
(Most children assured her that it went to live somewhere else based on their experience with horseshoe crabs.)
BW: (She carefully pointed to the ridges in the backbone of the top half of the shell.) Do you see these bumps? Do they remind you of anything?
CHILD 1: They're like these bumps in my back.
CHILD 2: Your backbone.
CHILD 1: Yes. That makes me think that what lived in that shell is dead.
BW: Dead?
CHILD 1: Yes, if I was somewhere and these bones in my back were somewhere else, I'd be dead.
BW: Well, lots of your friends think the animal is still alive.
CHILD 1: I think it's dead.
BW: I think you've got something very important there.

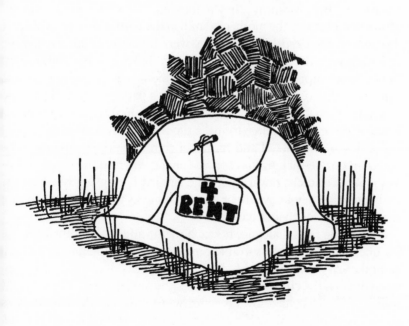

By isolating some qualities of good questions, it is possible to see what an important role they play in a visit to a natural history museum. First, questions asked of a child need to be answerable from the child's experience. Second, questions must appear to be worthwhile in the mind of the child. For example, the question, "What kind of animal do you think that is?" opens the possibility of these acceptable answers: "A mean animal." "A sea animal." "A big animal." The child did not have to know the name of the animal to answer the question correctly. "I wonder how this bear died?" is a good question because it exercises the imagination and does not rely on repetitions of memorized facts.

In contrast, notice how empty this question sounds: "What is the name of that animal?" This type of question only gathers information. While gathering information is useful, schools are full of this kind of activity. One of the wonderful qualities of museums is that they are places to think and to wonder, not necessarily to rehearse answers.

Thinking about natural history and asking the right questions also means confronting the unexpected and rejoicing in the puzzles nature has given us. At an exhibit of marine life, one mother was explaining to her child how barnacles are dead things attached to ships. The child peered through a magnifying glass embedded in the glass wall of the aquarium. "But, Mommy, they're moving," the child exclaimed with confusion. Hastily, the mother examined the barnacles only to observe that indeed the dead-looking things were in fact opening and closing and were very much alive. The mother's thinking was totally upset. "They're not supposed to do that," she announced excitedly. Here was a puzzle, a different way of thinking about a part of nature. Both child and adult then began to solve the puzzle by looking for a docent, a label, or some other source to make the puzzle less confusing.

Puzzles are the bread and butter of thinking. Museum-goers who rejoice in puzzle-making and puzzle-solving will find their natural history visit extremely rewarding. The reward is in using questions to find out what they know about it and their eyes to discover what they can figure out for themselves.

During the next dialogue, notice how the adult takes time to frame the question and offer a solvable puzzle to the child. Children bring a natural clarity to their world. The adult in the conversation shows interest in what the child knows and takes the time to listen. Once a child realizes that what he knows is worthwhile and that the parent cares about his opinion, his self-confidence soars. Meanwhile, all the ele-

ments of problem-solving,—thinking, interacting with others, finding
sources of information— have become second nature to the child.

CHILD: What is that?
ADULT: Yes, what is that? Let's look.
CHILD: Looks like a bird.
ADULT: Hmmm, it does look like a bird.
CHILD: Is it real?
ADULT: I think it was once alive, but I don't think it's alive now.
CHILD: Me neither because it's not breathing.
ADULT: Look at its eyes.
CHILD: They look like marbles, but those feathers are real.
ADULT: I wonder why they put it here?
CHILD: Because if it weren't here, we'd never see it; and it's
pretty.

Another characteristic of a good question is that it changes one's perspective. The Calvert Marine Museum has a crosscut diorama of nearby Calvert Cliffs. The change in perspective stimulates curiosity and inspires the child to think in a hypothetical way. Questions such as, "I wonder what the creek looks like without water?" or "What if this snake were loose, where would it go?" cause the answerer to step back and reassemble what he already knows. Taking new perspectives on old ideas or principles is a skill used by historians and scientists. They assemble their known facts and then take different points of view in hopes of finding new insights and making more accurate predictions.

Be aware that good questions often follow an illogical path. Try not to edit out a child's digressions because the museum offers a freedom in asking questions that the school does not. In the next example, seven-year-old Rebecca and her father examine a hawk. They allow themselves to deviate from the subject, to enjoy their discovery, and play with their thoughts. During the conversation, notice how her father simply describes or restates what Rebecca sees. It is clear that Rebecca is thinking hard about hawks.

The Hawk

The scene: On the shelf approximately five feet from the floor sat an enormous hawk. Its wings were extended, its eyes shining, poised for flight, but still as a rock. Seven-year-old Rebecca stared at the hawk, her father at her side.

REBECCA: Is that dead?
DAD: It isn't moving.
REBECCA: Is it real?
DAD: Its feathers look real.
REBECCA: But its eyes are too shiny.
DAD: Its claws look real.
REBECCA: What is it?
DAD: What do you think it is?
REBECCA: I think it's a mean bird.
DAD: What makes you think it's mean?
REBECCA: Look at its lips.
DAD: Pretty sharp.
REBECCA: Look at its feet.
DAD: They could scratch.
REBECCA: Here's its name. . . . .hawk. (She found the name

plate and sounded the word out.)

DAD: How do you think it got here?

REBECCA: It died.

DAD: It looks like it wasn't broken when it died.

REBECCA: Maybe it hit a window? Remember that bird that flew into our window?

DAD: What do you think it eats?

REBECCA: Other birds.

DAD: What makes you think that?

REBECCA: Its claws and its lips.

DAD: Yes, that beak looks like it bites hard and cuts.

Questions about natural history may come and go, but there is one question constantly on the mind of young children, "Is it real?" Every child who visits a natural history museum runs through a maze of questions about the stuffed animals on display. "Are they real?" "Were they alive at one time?" "How did they die?" "What does 'stuffed' really mean?"

Mike Campbell, Exhibit Curator at the Cape Cod Museum of Natural History, has helped many children out of this maze when he takes time to describe how a live hawk came to sit on the shelf. He explains how specimens come to museums from all kinds of sources—hit by cars, found in the wild, victims of malnutrition. Children who have begun to struggle with the issue of dead versus alive find it reassuring to know that animals are not simply murdered and placed on display.

The "Is it real?" question is very important to children. Talking about the "stuffed world" versus the living world enables the adult and child to go beyond standing in front of displays reading scientific names and remarking, "Oh, gosh."

Children go through stages of wondering about the "stuffed world." One three-year-old girl asked to wait by the stuffed ostrich display for a second egg to hatch. Her mother and father began a discussion about how the egg is not real. "See, the egg is not alive and the ostrich is not alive. It was alive once, but now it is stuffed." Agreeing to wait no longer, the little girl turned the corner to see the Eskimo exhibit and quite logically asked if these people were stuffed.

By four years of age, some children recognize that the birds were stuffed because that is the only way they can be seen and preserved. Not all children approach the "stuffed world" with such candor or confidence. One five-year-old boy adamantly refused to enter a room of stuffed birds. Unmasked fear covered his face. The accompanying adult tried several tactics to reassure him that they were in no danger of being attacked. Then, the adult even walked in the room to demonstrate that not one feather twitched. Finally, after a long silence, the little boy asked hesitantly, "Would they put stuffed boys in here?" The adult could now understand that the child had made the connection between stuffed birds and live birds but was mystified by how and why the act of stuffing happened. The adult happily reassured the boy that never would a museum put a stuffed boy on display and, further, if he crossed into the room, he would be in no danger of being stuffed.

The "stuffed world" mystifies many children. Consequently, adults can benefit from exploring a child's understanding about stuffed birds. The act of stuffing animals and life-death issues, such as how four lion cubs came to be stuffed with their mother, are always at the forefront of their curiosity. Dozens of curators at natural history museums agree that, "Is it real?" is the most often asked question. Answer that question and the child and adult can open the doors to many more discoveries.

Sharing

When an adult and child choose to visit a natural history museum or zoo, they are sharing a love of nature together. While learning about children's questions prepares an adult for sharing the exploration, the other side of this process—the answer or lack of an answer—needs to be addressed.

When a child asks a question, the adult must choose to share information or share confusion. Chapter Two touched on how important it is for adults to withhold information in order to share in the joy of discovery.

When children ask, "What is that?" a parent can of course tell them, "It's a white-crowned sparrow." Many adults and children, however, benefit from a little hand-holding. Several previous examples in this chapter described successful discoveries because of the types of questions asked and because the adult understood a child's basic need to figure out a problem. The child who shows his parent how much he knows about Hopi Indians is happier than the child who just listens to the parent read from the accompanying plaque. Given the opportunity and the time, a child can usually solve a problem on his own.

It is sometimes difficult for an adult to know when to withhold answers and let a child try to figure it out, and when to offer clues. One docent says, "I always want the kids to win. I give them enough information so that they can logically find the answer."

When adults decide to share information, it is easier to do it in a sneaky, almost subtle way than in a way that says, "I'm telling you this now." At the end of the hawk example used earlier in this chapter, Rebecca was gently taught about a bird's beak. This fact was given to her in context in language that she had already used. There are many ways to share this kind of information without going to the extent of saying, "Birds don't have lips, birds have beaks." This latter statement diminishes the quality of what the child knows by implying that what the child says is *wrong*.

Sharing the confusion of nature with a child accomplishes two things. First, the child often rallies to help the parent locate the answer and, second, the parent and child enjoy a wonderful time together. During a recent visit to the National Museum of Natural History, one mother pointed to a life-sized display of Indian children playing a hoop and spear game. The mother simply said, "I can't figure this game out." The two boys accompanying her rushed to her aid.

BOY 1: Well, this ring is like a net.
BOY 2: Yes, see, they throw the stick through the net.
MOM: No, I don't see.
BOY 1: OK. Do you have anything that's a circle?
MOM: A quarter.
BOY 1: No, just a circle, not a dot.
MOM: My key ring.
BOY 2: Roll it on the floor.
MOM: Why?
BOY 2: Just roll it and watch.
MOM: OK.
(As she rolled it along the floor, the boys zestily tossed imaginary spears through the circle.)
BOY 1: See, Indians had to shoot animals with spears for their food. Kids had to become good at it. So they played this game. Now do you see?

Actually acting out the game made it more real in everyone's mind. For many children who enjoy "doing" while they are thinking instead of "just thinking," being able to demonstrate the game provided them with the chance to test their imagination.

Parents often find they are afraid to share too much confusion. After all, at some point the child is going to wonder what, in fact, the adult does know. In an effort to find out what children thought about adults not knowing all the answers, a docent asked several children one day if they thought she was stupid because the children had to teach her about so many things.

ADULT: There are so many things you have taught me. Do you think I'm stupid?
SONDRA (age 6): No!
ADULT: But when there are so many things I don't know, isn't that stupid?
SONDRA: No, stupid people are the ones who think they know it all.
MATTHEW (age 6): No, smart people look to find out more.
BETH: No one knows everything.

In these responses it is evident that these children are blissfully unaware that they live in a culture where adults believe it is their duty to teach children everything they need to know. Most children feel that adults can turn to them for help in learning new things, but the truth is that children rarely have a chance to show what they know. By allowing a child the time to figure something out and share it with the adult, the child becomes conscious of becoming a creatively and spontaneously thinking being.

From the Adult's Perspective

Most natural history museums hold thousands and sometimes millions of samples in their collection. Of the number chosen for display by the museum, one can expect to think about only a few dozen at the most during one visit. Adults have had years to learn how to focus and edit out stimuli. Children rarely reduce the world in this fashion. Therefore, adults who do not want the visit to fail will be eager to look for ways to keep the museum or zoo from seeming overwhelming to the child.

Adults need to avoid two classic museum mistakes. First, do not overwhelm the child with facts. In their enthusiasm for natural history, many museum-goers become fact-consumers. The old routine, "We're going to learn things," begins. While learning facts is a valid reason for going, a child has probably consumed his quota of natural history facts early into the visit. The child's consumption of facts may overwhelm his desire to do and see things during the remainder of the visit.

An adult needs to take a careful inventory of what there is to do to avoid overpowering a child. Many families call ahead to find out about special exhibits or register for special activities such as the Smithsonian's Discovery Room (National Museum of Natural History.) By limiting the area to be covered and, at the same time, remaining open to the odd exhibit, the adult can keep fatigue and frustration at bay. Places like zoos and aquariums offer such diversity that the promise of visiting again and again satisfies even the most energetic four-year-old who wants to do it all in one day.

The other classic mistake adults often make is to violate a basic museum-going right which states that all museum-goers have the right to their own interests. Adults are often weighted down with a hierarchy of interests that places a higher value on rare and unusual creatures. Ironically, many children find all creatures rare and wonderful. Imagine a mother who has set aside the afternoon for a visit to the zoo with her three-year-old. The mother tries to explain that the zoo is a place filled with exotic animals, animals who will never cross the path by the house. To the mother's horror the three-year-old rushes past the giraffes, past the zebras, past the hippos, past the elephants, and chases the pigeons. The little girl squeals with delight as the pigeons take flight at her approach. What the mother fails to realize is that no other living creature takes flight when the three-year-old approaches. It is no wonder that the pigeons are beguiling. The most important and not-to-be-overlooked factor is that the child has begun a life journey of loving to go to the zoo. In time, the elephant and the seals will capture her attention, but for the mother to demand or expect the elephants to win her three-year-old's attention today is shortsighted. It is much better for the child and adult to enjoy whatever attracts the child's interest. The child then learns to trust her own responses to the world.

Because of the large size of many natural history sites, one of the hardest parts of the visit is knowing when to stop. Adults need to be alert to the child's signs of fatigue. Two hours is the maximum time suggested for any museum. Outdoor nature activities, such as a zoo,

can be all-day affairs because there is more movement and variation in this type of activity.

While determining the length of the visit is important in setting limits, it is the pace of the visit that gives life to the visit. Be attuned to the child's curiosity and do not rush. Rushing always ruins a museum visit. If there is limited time, then make the child aware that only so much time is available. Do not nudge the child to the point where everything becomes a blur. In reality, it is not physically or psychologically possible to see everything.

For adults, the final concern at a natural history museum or nature location is the child's personal safety. The rules at the zoo and aquarium need to be explained and followed. Hands-on discovery rooms and local nature centers are good opportunities to touch things; however, porcupine quills are sharp, wood gives slivers, and shells can break. In addition, live animals require respect and instructions on how to hold them. Unlike stuffed animals, live animals cannot be dropped or poked without endangering their lives. While encouraging a child to locate their *Furry Me's* or *Reptilian Me's* in nature, the adult needs to keep one eye out for a child's safety in case the differences between what a child imagines nature to be like and the reality of nature turns out to require bandages or the drying of tears.

Post-Visit Activities

The great thing about natural history is that it is everywhere. The backyard, the neighborhood, and the surrounding community offer endless opportunities to apply what one has learned at the museum. Observing squirrels or pigeons on the street or in the park is an example of such an opportunity in everyday life. Another is looking at the layers of dirt when planting spring flowers or uncovering worms and bugs under rocks. These experiences allow the child to see that nature can be found in every square inch of his yard.

Many children are inspired to start their own collections of "stuff" when they return from the natural history museum. Leaves, rocks, and insects can be easily examined by parent and child. The same type of questioning process described previously in this chapter can bring the child to the point where he or she can classify and compare the stone from the driveway with the stone from the neighbor's garden.

After visiting natural history museums, most families are aware of how much their world has changed. One activity for examining change in the world is to compare maps of some part of their world to show the impact of development. For example, a variety of topological maps would show how the land has been physically changed by roads, houses, and buildings. These changes can be seen every day. When a new house is built or the child notices a bulldozer carving out another lane of highway, these observations demonstrate that natural history is not something locked away in a case at the museum or a cage at the zoo.

There are many home experiments in which a child can see natural history in the making. For instance, if a child wonders how the museum can figure out what a dinosaur looks like when there are no photographs, one activity might be making imprints in clay or plaster of paris and then determining what can be observed from just the impressions. One mother gave her children the bones of a boiled chicken wing and asked the children to see if they could figure out how the bones went together. In this way a child begins to really look at bones and understand that, from just a few bones, an expert can make guesses regarding what an animal looked like.

If a child has shown interest in a particular animal or subject, stop at the gift shop to check their resources. Libraries and bookstores are also

good follow-up activities. These resources allow the child to review what he has seen. Depending on a family's location, wildlife refuges and nature centers offer living histories of the animal kingdom.

Wonderers of the World

It is easy to take nature for granted. The wonders of the world, however small or large, present young and old wonderers with a new respect for nature. It is worth remembering that museums, zoos, arboretums, and nature centers are worlds unto themselves. Yes, they are oases and wonderlands; but more incredibly, they are places of inspiration, places to go to get excited about the world. There, the family can watch the beaver and giggle about his teeth, enjoy his multicolored brown coat, and admire his diligence. As they consider the beaver, they can talk, laugh, or be silent. They can rejoice in what they know and celebrate when they find puzzles to solve. Activities that honor natural history, whether it is puzzling about stuffed birds or searching for fossils along a cliff, build an awareness that families are part of the wonder that is the natural world.

Chapter Five
History Museums: The Saving Place

*"A man said: 'Thou tree!' The tree answered with the same scorn.
'Thou Man! Thou art greater than I only in thy possibilities.' "*

—Stephen Crane, *Legends III*

A history museum is a place where the reality of the past is restored through the surviving evidence. Visiting history museums and historical sites enables the family to see that certain events really did happen and that the famous personalities really did live. Without the uniforms or weapons, the tools and machines, or the toys and home furnishings that are collected by museums, the people and places that make up our social and political legacy seem like elements in another tall tale.

When a family goes in search of a *History Me* at a history museum or historical site, there are special considerations that contribute to how rewarding their visit will be. Adults must understand that a child's concept of history is just beginning. This chapter identifies these concerns and suggests ways the family can expand their enjoyment of history through the different types of history visits.

Children and History: Three Basic Questions

When a family first considers visiting the history museum or historical site, one of the first questions that arises is whether children understand history. Children are indeed capable of understanding history, but it must be defined in their terms. Children have neither the depth of experiences nor the background information that adults have when they go to history museums. What they do have is a rich repository of personal experiences that they can use to relate to history. Young children, ages three to nine, bring to history their feelings, their senses, and their thoughts. They find *Owner Me's*, *Wagon Train Me's*, and *Playing Me's* to name just a few. Through this personal approach, children incorporate the ideas and deeds of the past into their own experience.

History is a record of what happened to people during another time. Many of the feelings that are part of an historical event are already present in childhood. Children know what it feels like to win or lose and to love or hate. Children have a big storehouse of these feelings. They build sand castles that they are enormously proud of and then destroy them with wild delight. When four-year-old Sally ties her shoes for the first time, family history has been made. Sally's landmark is typical of how most children personalize history. When Sally hears that famous figures of history are often famous because they did something for the first time, Sally can identify with how proud those figures must have felt. Beginning at an early age, children know all about fairness and honor and loyalties to friends and siblings. Beyond this basic commonality of thought and feeling, the history in history museums offers clues as to what happens when people act certain ways and venture to new frontiers.

How much history children understand is another issue that concerns a history museum visit. The older the child, the more history he

or she is able to digest. Adults have lived, thought, and made sense of
the world for a longer time than their children; therefore, they have
developed a greater supply of subtle understandings such as symbolic
thinking, a sense of historical importance, and chronological time.

Adults have cultivated a sense of chronological time that synthesizes
and orders events. They know that the Civil War was fought after the
Revolutionary War and that Abe Lincoln lived long before John Ken-
nedy. This sense of chronological time is the product of many years of
talking, studying, and reading. Sometime around the age of four, children begin to get a sense of chronological time when they can imagine a
time "before now."

Another subtle understanding of history that increases with age is
the use of historical symbols. At fairly young ages, children begin to
think in symbols. In modern America, a child understands that the
golden arches "stand for" hamburgers and french fries. By age six, a
child learns that the letters c-a-t "stand for" their furry little friend.
These examples are all evidence of children's symbolic thinking. During a history visit the important issue to remember is that symbols have
different meanings to a child than to an adult. A flag is a classic symbol
of a nation. When an adult sees an American flag, it is likely that the
flag symbolizes the freedoms and rights and what it costs to maintain
those freedoms. However, a child has fewer meanings to bring to the
flag. A six-year-old might simply associate the flag with the place
where he lives.

What are children going to find interesting about history? This last
question is very important because many adults are concerned that
their children are not going to be interested in anything except whether
it is time for lunch. The surprising thing about children and history
museums is that children are drawn naturally to the "big" ideas of history, not the little details. Both children and adults have limited abilities to ingest facts; therefore, when a family considers a pair of boots in
a glass case, they are not going to be very interested unless they find
out something "big" about them. What are the qualities of the boots
that bring out its bigness? Is it the owner's name or the valor of the
general who wore them during the Civil War? In most cases, it does not
make much of a difference to a young child if their grandmother is not
as old as George Washington. Both are people who belong to the past.
What interests most children is not that George Washington is 200

years older than their grandmother, but that George Washington wore false teeth that made him irritable.

The ability to imbue items with value and to appreciate the "bigness" of history is evident in very young children. Just as they recognize that their special blanket is not "just any blanket," they are able to realize that a pair of boots is not "just anybody's boots." Artifacts achieve that larger-than-life quality when a human connection can be found. Telling the stories of how children used certain items, reading books that relate a part of the history, or attending special events all help the family make those human connections. Sometimes these connections can become quite profound. One five-year-old child wondered after a tour of the home of Robert E. Lee how a man of his importance and greatness could be on the losing side of a war.

While history museums can be very exciting to children, families may need extra help in finding something interesting. Hard and "big" questions can trigger an interest in artifacts. Looking at history and trying to make sense of it can lead to hard and seemingly unpleasant questions. Children appreciate adults who are willing to explore any issue even if it is difficult or unpleasant. A child who asks his mother, "Why do little children die in grown-up wars?" has begun to look at history as a source of answers in a confusing world. If children start thinking that children of the past are like them, then history is answering some of those unpleasant questions that come up in everyday life. These are the kinds of questions that cause children to learn about history. Their attraction to history museums is very clear when they discover the museum holds answers to some questions.

Before starting a history museum visit, it is a good idea for adults to take a moment to consider how the whole family views history. Even a child who has previous knowledge about a historical site from books or school needs to know that it is not what he knows that is important as much as how his adult companion values his thoughts. The adult who is waiting for a child to get his dates straight has overlooked the opportunity for the family has to think about larger issues. Knowing that children are capable of understanding history, of placing values on history, and of tackling the "big" ideas of history frees the history visit from getting tangled up in facts.

Types of History Visits

There are basically three types of history visits: reenactments of historical events, historic homes, and traditional museums. All three categories are equally capable of inspiring and fascinating children and adults. To take advantage of each particular type of visit, it is helpful for the family to know some of the special considerations that will affect their ability to find their *History Me's*.

Reenactments

Reenactments are special events where battles are refought, recipes remixed, and engines restarted. They allow the child to see how tools were used, weapons were fired, and fields were tilled. Instead of listening or watching movies about how the Indians did beadwork, children can see an Indian woman beading a belt. All the child's senses participate. Hearing, smelling, touching, and seeing these kinds of events etch them in the child's memory very powerfully. With children up to the age of seven, it is very important for them to understand that the event is really "pretend." This is especially true for reenactments that involve pain and suffering. Adults need to explain that all the participants have worked very hard to make this reenactment seem like a real battle. The soldiers moaning in the field are not dying or really in pain; rather they are just pretending. When adults simply state that a reenactment is not real, children can be confused. A young child interprets these real people doing real things, saying real words, and carrying real guns as reality. The following example shows what can happen at reenactments when children do not understand this special pretend kind of reality.

A family with two girls, ages four and five, gathered their picnic dinner, drove to a Civil War battlefield, and awaited an "evening reenactment" of the famous battle. Darkness fell. Every effort had been made to create "living history." The family, led by a guide with a flashlight, trudged through the tall grass to meet different soldiers who dramatically shared their tales of war. The old stone house was lit by lanterns and the smell of acrid medicine filled the air. Wounded, moaning soldiers lay in each room. A doctor lamented on his mounting work and dwindling energies.

Any adult who has ever read about the Civil War was soaring with delight and murmuring, "Oh this must have been terrible." The two young girls, however, looked with increasingly alarm at the moaning soldiers and the blood-stained rags wrapped loosely around their heads, legs, and arms. They dashed to the room where the doctor sat seemingly exhausted. The believability of the situation spawned anguish within the girls until the four-year-old pulled on her mother's coat and said, "Why aren't we doing anything?"

At this point, the parents quickly realized the confusion of realities and began to explain how these men were not really in pain. Once the parents talked about pretending, the girls began to relax. While a reenactment is a marvelous visual aid, it gives a sense of reality that movies or television cannot bring. Being in the middle of real people who are convincingly recreating human misery can cause anxiety in a four-year-old child.

Once a child understands that the reenactment is just pretending, the child can enjoy the show. With children younger than six, however, it is questionable how much history they are learning. Even though the original event occurred in the past, this recreated event is clearly taking place in the present in the child's mind.

Reenactments take another form with hands-on history rooms. At these places children are allowed to examine historical objects by trying on clothing, rebuilding buckets, or perhaps weaving chair seats. Conversation at those times between the child and the docent or adult offers the child a chance to picture the past. When a child turns nine or ten and studies colonial life, his understanding of colonial history may begin with how he once fitted a bucket together or wove a seat for a chair. Hands-on history rooms give the tools and toys of yesterday the dynamics of interaction that books and television cannot attain.

Historic Homes

Historic homes present a way for a family to recapture the people in history. There are four major sources of information at a historic home that can provide clues regarding how people once lived: the house itself, the docents who give tours, the history of the people who once lived in the house, and participation in special holiday events.

Because a family has a home and therefore a point of reference in history, a visit to a historic home is a good way to make observations about how home life has changed dramatically. The whole family can make comparisons between the past and present. The idea that the past was different from today is a big idea for three-year-olds. Large middle halls were characteristic of all homes in the Federal and Victorian periods. Most homes today do not have the luxury of roomy entrance ways. Children can generate ideas about how their lives are different from those of the people who lived in houses like Monticello or Gunston Hall. Taking the time to think about the rooms in the house, or where the toys were stored, or how water was brought into the house helps a child to imagine what it was like to live in these historic homes. For instance, when a room completely devoted to music is found, children can compare the importance of music to this colonial family to the importance of the television or stereo system in their own home. This thinking and comparing helps children avoid getting caught in a flood of facts and allows the family to find value in what is being preserved.

Tours of historic homes given by trained docents is another source of history and another way to bring the historic home to life. Most docents have their favorite tales about the people who have lived in a particular historic house. Rumors of ghosts, family parties, or mischievous children all contribute to the history of an historic home. When adults and children seek out these tales from the docent, they can visualize the story better.

Often, a family can create anticipation about an upcoming visit to an historic site or home by telling and reading stories that include historical facts and focus on some of the "big" issues. Four-year-old Nathan had been told the story of Lincoln's assassination several times. On an outing with house guests to Ford's Theater, Nathan took up the role of storyteller-guide. His story, which follows, was full of action and excitement and he obviously took great joy from the telling of it.

"John Wilkes Booth. He hated Lincoln. He sneaked in. Walked across the back. Kicked in the door. He was there earlier. Lincoln didn't know. Booth shot him and jumped. Caught his spur in the Treasury flag and broke his leg. He was a gymnast and could have made that jump—-but his spur caught in the flag and he fell. John Wilkes Booth knew about plays. He picked a part where everyone was laughing so they wouldn't hear the shot."

Knowing that story in advance and being able to tell it to the guests made Nathan aware of how he could participate in the stories that make up history. During the visit the family and the guests retraced John Wilkes Booth's path. They walked up the stairs, around the back, saw Lincoln's chair, and viewed the stage from up there. Standing there, they could see their *Gymnastic Me* leaping from the balcony and their *Detective Me* calculating how Booth would have exited the theatre. If a child knows the order of events, especially the events of such a powerful, dramatic story, his willingness to participate in the telling or recreation of the history is greater.

The other way to cultivate an interest in a historic home is to attend special events such as holiday celebrations. Candlelight tours or the making of period crafts and foods create a living history where children can easily see the difference between then and now. At many historic homes several seasonal or holiday celebrations are planned. A wide range of activities can be experienced from tasting 19th-century ice cream flavors in the summer to wassailing during Christmas. Call the location in advance to check on upcoming events and make reservations if necessary.

Traditional Museums

In contrast to the action that occurs at reenactments and to a lesser extent at historic homes, a traditional history museum cannot offer movement and activities as lures into history. Here, history is placed inside cases and behind ropes. Whatever the subject of the history, the success of this type of history visit depends on the imagination and thinking skills of the visitor. Imagination is needed for adults and children to create visions in their heads of how things were made and then used. As mentioned earlier in this chapter, it is important to realize that these visions of the past will not necessarily be identical. Regardless of which vision is more accurate or creative, it is essential that all visions are equally valued.

This discussion includes the social and political histories of a culture such as the National Museum of American History, as well as museums that document a culture's science and technology. The most popular museum in Washington, the National Air and Space Museum, is more accurately a history of man's adventure into the sky, and less a science museum as defined in Chapter Six.

The prerequisite of the history museum visit is the same as that for art and natural history museums. That is, a child has an adult companion who is interested in what the child thinks and is willing to listen. One helpful role the adult can take during a history museum visit is one where he can limit the exhibit or focus on one particular aspect. Because of the large quantity of things to see at major history museums, it is easy for families to start wandering and overextend their energies. Whenever possible, it is a good idea to have the family concentrate its energies on one object or a series of objects. A loom is a difficult machine to explain to children without actually touching it or seeing it operate. The explanation of what stays in place, what moves, and how it moves is dizzying for adults, let alone children. Here is how one family looked more deeply at a loom located behind a glass case.

BONNIE (eight-years-old): What is that?

ADULT: A weaving loom.

BONNIE: To make clothes on?

ADULT: Yes.

JOHN (six years old): How does it work?

ADULT: Look, some threads go this way and others cross them.

BONNIE: Oh, yea.

ADULT: Look at your shirt. Do you see threads crossing?

JOHN: I can see threads. Look, some go this way and some go that way.

ADULT: So, once people made cloth like this?

BONNIE: Yes. There weren't any stores to buy clothes.
ADULT: Are you telling me they threaded all those threads for
one piece of cloth?
BONNIE: That's right.
ADULT: I guess it took a long time.
JOHN: I bet they didn't have a lot of clothes.

When Bonnie asked about the loom, she immediately created the
opportunity and the reason to talk about the loom. The adult realized
that explaining the loom included more than just clothmaking. With
the statement, "Look at your shirt," the adult set up the experience for
the children to share what they knew. The adult was able to help the
children find the *Weaver Me* that was present. Through simple observations about the cloth of the child's shirt, the children were able to
discover the significance of the loom by themselves. The adult chose
not to go beyond saying, "Look at your shirt," although he knew how
looms worked and who used them. Instead, he showed a willingness to
be taught by the children. This is the main difference between offering
to focus an exhibit and telling about it. When a child finds the answer
to what matters about the loom by himself, his sense of ownership of
that knowledge is very strong.

It is possible that a child at any age can walk into a history museum
and be fascinated by the first artifact that he sees. If a child is immediately engaged or interested, the best thing any adult can do is join in the
interest and enjoy the moment. Some children at very early ages are
fascinated by history museums and need no help getting interested or
understanding what they are seeing. It is also possible that young children, four-year-olds to ten-year-olds, may not be equipped to sustain
interest in historical exhibits.

The following discussion on Ways of Looking can be very useful to
adults who are looking for a framework or plan while visiting the museum instead of wandering from exhibit to exhibit hoping the child will
encounter an artifact that will interest him.

Ways of Looking

As in all museums, random wandering has a tendency to erode energy in adults and children. There are three ways of looking at history
museums with children: the Treasure Hunt, Working as an Historian,
and the Detective. All of these offer structure and a sense of accom-

plishment to museum-goers. Each way of looking must be personalized by each family during each visit depending upon family ages, interests, and energy levels.

The Treasure Hunt

The Treasure Hunt is a very basic way of looking at history. It works well with traditional history museums. It is a simple approach that can be adapted to children of all ages. For example, a list of appropriate treasures for three- and four-year-olds can be compiled by calling the education office of the history museum the family intends to visit. Ask for five artifacts that young children would enjoy and their locations within the museum. Upon arrival at the museum, the adult can secure maps of the building and the intrepid adventurers begin their search!

Finding the treasured objects becomes a quest. There is a sense of accomplishment when all the objects are found. The structure of this type of visit prevents a history museum from becoming an endless parade of exhibits that quickly wears down a three-year-old's ability to enjoy.

By ages five and six a child may be ready to look for five related objects in a treasure hunt. When a child is in pursuit of five Civil War or Revolutionary War treasures, he may become familiar with how the museum classifies history. Certainly seven-year-olds can find the search worthwhile for five artifacts to save in case of fire. In the process of deciding what to save, adults and children find themselves adjusting their values, searching for added information, supporting ideas, and persuading people to change their minds. All of these skills touch at the very heart of daily living. When an eight-year-old decides to save the Star Spangled Banner, he discovers feelings of loyalty that he may never have known previously.

As a way of looking at history, the treasure hunt is an excellent way to introduce the whole family to a new museum. Treasure hunts are fun and not demanding for the adult or child. They can also lead the family to places where the *Curious Me's* might not normally be found.

Working as an Historian

Another successful way of looking at history is to try to simulate the work of an historian. Historians use their knowledge of the world, sift through the evidence that has survived, investigate the different points of view of the past, and then arrive at an understanding about what might have happened originally.

A family has all the same tools available to the historian. This chapter has already shown how much children know and, when given a chance, how much they can observe. Some people may doubt that children are capable of understanding how a person's point of view influences history. Within a six-year-old's experience, however, is the likelihood of having participated in a team sport.

A soccer match is a good example of how families are already familiar with personal points of view and how they can influence or distort what is seen and heard. One point of view is represented by the father of the boy whose team is winning. Another point of view is put forth by the parent of the losing team who mistrusts the referee. A completely different point of view is recorded by one player who is riveted to an astonishing ant hill over by the goal. If a historian were to record the game, how would its history be fairly and accurately told?

Once the six-year-old soccer player sees how the soccer game changes according to the point of view, he can begin to understand how point of view affects other parts of his daily life. The disparity among three separate versions of a soccer game is similar to the disparity a historian must consider when attempting to record history. As children grow older, they can appreciate that what a museum or a reenactment presents can only be one point of view. Historians are continually faced with conflicting evidence and differing points of view. They must use their knowledge to try to present the most accurate and objective point of view possible. Children who recognize in their daily lives that there are often conflicting points of view besides their own are beginning to do the work of historians.

The analogy of the soccer game is an important one because it directly touches a child's life and the issues of point of view and fairness. Point of view and fairness are not only issues found in the current world but also have been important issues historically. The following conversation which took place at the National Portrait Gallery demonstrates how knowledgeable children can be when they are helped to examine differing points of view. In order to take a close look at the thinking behind what seems like a casual conversation, the conversation will be presented first as it occurred and then synopsized with comments that underline the careful reasoning behind what the adult said.

One morning at the National Portrait Gallery, a museum of art and history, a five-, a six-, and a seven-year-old bounded out of the elevator followed by their adult companions for a morning tour. Many Civil War portraits and busts were on display. Immediately, Sondra spotted a bust and portrait of John Brown.

SONDRA: Look, these two are of the same man.

ADULT: Yes, they are.

SONDRA: (looking at the bust) He's in trouble. That rope around his chest looks creepy.

BETH: He looks mean and sad, too.

MATTHEW: You can't tell if he's white or black 'cause it's made of that black stuff.

BETH: His hair looks like he doesn't comb it.

ADULT: What about the painting; it looks different.

SONDRA: He's in a dungeon; look how dark it is behind him.

MATTHEW: He's white. I think he's a robber because he's poor and can't comb his hair and he's in jail.

ADULT: Let's see. He's in trouble. Maybe in jail. Maybe poor. Maybe he robs. He's got a rope around his neck. Do you think he's old?

MATTHEW: Oh yea. Look at his hair and eyes.

ADULT: (Standing up, recognizing that lighting is preventing the children from seeing many details and lifting the children for a better look) Can you see more now?

SONDRA: Oh wow, look at his hand. There's something on it, maybe a handcuff.

BETH: Yea, look at his eyes. He's sad.

ADULT: Shall we check this plaque to see how much we figured out on our own?

CHILDREN: Okay.

ADULT: It says he was against slavery. It says he lived before the Civil War. What was that war about?

BETH: Was that with England?

MATTHEW: No, it was the North and South.

BETH: Oh yes, that's right.

SONDRA: The North was the good team and the South was the bad team.

ADULT: How did they know who was good and who was bad?

MATTHEW: They announced it at the beginning.

ADULT: Oh, well. This is very confusing then because John Brown was against slavery. Now that seems good to me, doesn't it to you?
EVERYONE: Yea.
ADULT: Well, he was against slavery and yet he was considered bad by some people.
MATTHEW: Abraham Lincoln was the leader of the North's team.
ADULT: Was he a good man?
SONDRA: Oh yes.
ADULT: Well, I don't quite understand. Abraham Lincoln and John Brown were both against slavery, yet they both were killed because other people thought they were bad.
MATTHEW: I think in a war everyone thinks they are on the good side.

The conversation appears to have gone rather quickly when, in fact, there were many long silences and a great deal of pondering by all the participants. The following explanation can help adults recognize the importance of taking time and phrasing questions to help children bring order to their reasoning.

When Sondra first stated, "look," she created a reason to notice something. The adult knelt down next to the children to have a look from their point of view. Remember, lighting can have a disastrous effect for those people who are taller or shorter than the adult norm. After the children had made some initial observations, the adult restated the information and thereby provided a frame for further discovery. Then he encouraged the children to go on with their look by asking a question that was easily answerable.

After all the children had had a look at the works from different points of view, the adult pointed to the plaque of information beside the portrait. When the adult asked if they were interested in seeing how much they had figured out, this affirmed each child's ability to decode a painting. If the adult had said, "Let's see what really happened," it would have denied all the children's hard work. If the adult had said, "Let's find the answer," then he would be implying that the answer to their question always lies somewhere other than inside ourselves. It is important to note that no child had asked the adult to read the plaque and that two of the children who were able readers were not interested in consulting the plaque. The obvious reason is that most children enjoyed piecing together puzzles by themselves. The adult asked permission to read the plaques. If the children had said no, then there would have been no need to read it. It would also indicate that the children were not interested and they were not ready to hear.

Next, the adult paraphrased the plaque to reaffirm the children's discoveries about John Brown: He was old, he was sad, and he was in trouble. Then the adult added new information when he mentioned the Civil War, choosing not to ask questions about chronological time but to pursue ideas. When one child referred to the North as a good team and the South as the bad team, the adult sensed that here was an analogy with which many children would be familiar. In addition, the adult knew that at this age a child's sense of right and wrong is more active than his sense of geography. Pursuing the topic of North and South could only be an exercise in acquiring more facts. In contrast, a child's feelings of fairness and good and evil are worthwhile topics to explore. When the adult consciously brought up the word "slavery" he was risking the fact that the children had already associated good or bad with the word "slavery." Responding to the hard question about Brown's beliefs, the children fell silent. When no one came forward with another question, the group of children moved on to another case.

Adults need to be very patient while children are trying to make sense of this complex situation. Although it is tempting to fill in the silence with explanations, children need time to think through big questions and to understand history on their terms. When silence occurs during a history museum visit, the family needs to treasure these moments of reflection and not mistake them for indifference or boredom.

Making new discoveries in thinking is an activity children do daily. In history museums, adults can join children in thinking by taking time to listen carefully, by noticing the earnest intent children possess when trying to solve a problem, and by being interested in the way children think. Points of view, fairness, and John Brown were all elements of some important discoveries about how we judge people and events. Young Matthew certainly captured some very respectable understanding of war that day at the National Portrait Gallery.

Looking for points of view and fairness is only part of the work of an historian. When families sift through artifacts looking for clues about what certain items meant to other cultures, they are taking the role of the archaeologist, a special kind of historian. Archaeologists must exerise their imaginations regarding how a tool was used or a toy played with. Recreating the natural habitat of an artifact provides a context where meaning can be found.

How do exhibits relate the native habitat of an era? Normally, the museum selects a background photograph or a range of related objects that includes scenery and typical environments where an object might be found. A recent exhibit on the popular culture figure, "Superman," is a good example.

What does the family expect to understand when they see replicas of the local drugstore where the comic book was sold? By placing original comic books and memorabilia beside the habitat where Superman flourished, the museum-goer can get a clearer idea of a different time, different furniture, different technology, different plumbing, and different sized rooms. Children rarely see their parents' homes the way they were decorated when their parents were children. Having a complete replica where adults from all over the country can find familiar sofas or lamps or sinks offers the adult an added excitement about sharing his childhood that may not be generated by a comic book in a glass case by itself. Museums are striving to create exhibits that increase talking among visitors and provide a backdrop for an exhibit such as that done for Superman. This exhibit illustrates how creating a natural habitat even for a fictitious character can be successful.

The Navy Museum in Washington is a fine example of the careful presentation of artifacts in their native habitat or in context. Two exhibits that are highly accessible for a family are the Submarine Room, where a complete interior of a submarine is available to visitors, and the Polar Exploration exhibit which recreates a completely outfitted tent in polar conditions. The museum clearly realizes that visitors, even dedicated ones, need help bringing unfamiliar objects to life. In this instance, panoramic photographs of the terrain showing snowshoes and other gear that was required for survival gives a context for the objects and makes them more real in the visitor's mind.

Museums that work to present native habitats do the work of the historian for us; but in some cases, the thrill lies in finding an object encased in glass without any setting and joining with a child to create its original environment. Viewing a set of 19th-century dental equipment could present an excellent opportunity to imagine what the dentist's office must have looked like, what the patient looked like and even the dentist himself. In recapturing the human element as well as the native habitat, historical artifacts can be brought to life in this way.

At a history museum, children have the chance to use their decoding skills just like the historian as they encounter objects separated from their native habitat. When three children came across an Indian rug with figures of people woven into it, they tried to make sense of the rug without any clues as to what the rug really meant. Whether their theories were accurate was essentially irrelevant because each child was able to give the artifact meaning by interpreting the symbols given to him. The worth in this activity is that children learn to value what they think and feel without being told what it "really" means. Their confidence in expressing what they think creates a positive environment for learning. When the children asked what the weaver meant by using certain shapes and symbols, then someone needed to help them find the historically accurate answer.

Historical artifacts also require a historian to think about the appearance of an artifact. Does the object look as if it has ever been fixed up or broken? Many people wonder why the museum does not repair an object before it is put on display. The dilemma for museum conservators is whether to restore an object and thereby diminish its historical value or display an item that appears damaged.

When objects are not perfectly preserved, there is usually a good reason. Historians look at the nicks in furniture and stains in the cloth as clues to the roles these objects played. A chair with nicks on one side might reveal that boot stirrups scratched it. The stains on an apron may give clues about what kinds of foods the family ate or how hard the woman of the house worked. There are many reasons why an object survives in a particular condition. When a family chooses to look at the torn pages and broken wheels of history, they begin to see the worth of preserving things as they were found, not as they may have looked before anyone used them.

From the Adult's Perspective

During the search for a *History Me* it is important for the adult to realize that the thinking and puzzling process that history generally inspires does not require a Master's degree in western civilization. Finding a *History Me* is not a matter of selecting subjects that might be alluring to a child. Most *History Me*'s are discovered when the adult is ready to contribute time and patience to this activity. In this chapter, it has been demonstrated that children thrive when given the opportunity to share what they know and think about history. The family muse-

um-visit succeeds when adults recognize that the family already possesses what they need to enjoy history—themselves.

Expectations play a part in each museum visit. Expecting that a child
will react to the history museum in a certain way is normal. If parents
are disappointed with their children when their expectation does not
match the actual outcome of the visit, the parents may have been shortsighted. Children show interest in many positive ways. When visits
take surprise detours, it is important for the adult to recognize the
worth of the child's natural curiosity. For example, at the National
Museum of American History, two five-year-old boys stood in front of
the Star Spangled Banner waiting for the flag to be revealed. The accompanying adults had read to the children Peter Spier's book, *The
Star Spangled Banner*, and talked about the flag as a national symbol.

All seemed well until the music finally began. As the painted protec-
tive cover started to move, the boys had the momentary illusion that
the entire museum had been transformed into a gigantic elevator and
everyone was being transported to the place where the flag was displayed. All the adults' careful background work was erased by the boys
wondering if the floor was moving. Although puzzled at the boys reaction, the adults turned to the information desk to obtain validation that
the floor did not move. It was important to honor what the children
were curious about and to build on their curiosity. Watching the intensity with which those boys were eyeing the floor made it clear to the
adults that their first priority was to solve the floor dilemma. These
adults showed patience and flexibility when their carefully thought-
out discussion was derailed by the possibility of a moving floor. Thirty
minutes later when the flag reappeared, their interest shifted from the
floor back to the flag. They eagerly shared the story of Fort McHenry,
the subject of Peter Spier's book, with several other visitors and the
visit proceeded with both children fully involved.

Post-Visit Activities

Before written history there were pictures and stories. Storytelling
was the only history many generations knew. Young children, who
also do not read or write fluently, rely on stories, pictures, and objects
to create images of a world other than today's. The retelling of the story
after a museum visit inscribes that story in the child's personal anthology of history.

Small children thrive on repetition. After a child arrives home from a museum, encourage him to share the "stories" he or she discovered during the visit. In addition, by repeating the stories of his personal life, a child develops an appreciation for remembering times past. "Tell it again, Daddy," is a commonly heard plea that signifies how children need to hear and tell the same stories over and over. Only the quality of scale differentiates a child's personal history from a major historical event.

Whenever or wherever the family discovers the stories of history, the family needs to take advantage of the situation. It is helpful to charge history with the action it once had, people packing pistols, or nations swallowing nations. Let the *Camper Me* puzzle over the bleached white tent of George Washington. Stir the blood of a five-year-old with Revolutionary War stories and the *Soldier Me* is sure to start struggling through the knee-deep snow with his feet wrapped in rags.

For older children, a valid post-visit activity is to find a simply written biography or autobiography of a historical figure. This type of book enhances the human quality, the *Me* in museums. A visit to a historical site can make young historians out of former Saturday morning cartoon addicts. Compiling a family history is a wonderful exercise in geography and genealogy for a reading child. When the child quizzes "Grandma" on how her family came to be in America, a family tree can be charted, a map drawn, or a story illustrated. It is easy for children to bring their *History Me's* home, when home is a place where children have access to family artifacts like "Grandpa's" Tom Mix cowboy scarf or someone who tells them the stories of how the neighborhood once looked.

The *Me* Makes History

When children realize that their own family consists of able-bodied history-makers, then they grow up to appreciate the history-makers of their civilization. Families who carry the keys of history find there is no door they cannot open. This chapter has presented a number of ways to look at history and find meaning in historical events and artifacts. History visits from reenactments to traditional collections give the family a sense of belonging—a set of directions by which they can explore other worlds and always find their way home.

Chapter Six
Science Museums: A Making Sense Place

"The whole of science is nothing more than a refinement of everyday thinking."

—Albert Einstein, *Physics and Reality*

C hildren consider science a great source of power during their journey to make sense of their world. While expressions and interpretations of art help children create visions of their world, a child's observations and calculations about science show how children can work *with* their world. As children increase their knowledge of how the world acts and reacts, they develop confidence in themselves and in what happens around them.

At a science museum, the family can step into the laboratory and figure out how and why the world makes sense. While the laws of the universe are apparent to the family every day—apples fall, mold grow in the refrigerator, and bees, unfortunately, sting—few families are able to make the connection between their lives and scientific theories. Science museums present families with the chance to establish some of those connections.

What is a Science Museum?

Once upon a time, museum-goers went to science and technology museums to glimpse rare and wonderful parts of the world "under glass." Specimens and experiments were carefully displayed so that they posed no risk to the visitor nor were they in danger of being damaged by curious and clumsy visitors. Lengthy explanations, graphs and photographs were exhibited to explain the phenomena of science and the wonders of technology. Although these museums usually offered the family regularly scheduled classes where participants were able to get their hands on some "real science," it was not until fairly recently that museums began to incorporate a hands-on approach to science in the exhibit hall itself.

One museum that illustrates the changes science museums have undergone is the Museum of Science in Boston. This museum pioneered many kinds of hands-on exhibits such as the invisible man in all his organic complexity and a scale that determined what a visitor would weigh on the moon. These early successes and the popularity of many other exhibits from similar institutions have created a new category of science museum featuring hands-on science rather than hands-off exhibits. The Museum of Science is now expanding beyond the traditionally recognized categories of biology, chemistry, and physics to include the social sciences. Recent comprehensive exhibits on China, Egypt, and India present museum-goers with the chance to participate in the crafts as well as the technologies of other countries. This trend indicates that science is no longer considered an isolated activity to be found only in the laboratory.

Today, when families enter a science museum, whether it is the Exploratorium in San Francisco or the Science Museum in London, they are greeted by science-savvy guides (sometimes clad in lab coats), who are eager to explain the mysteries of the world from electricity to water to solar power. All the family is encouraged to get involved. Instead of talking or reading about technologically innovative exhibits the family can explore how bridges support weight and pumps circulate water. These exhibits are designed to allow the visitor to participate in some aspect of the principle or property of a phenomenon. Other types of science museums like aquariums, briefly mentioned in Chapter Four, now encourage visitors (with some guidance) to handle crabs and lobsters safely. In planetariums, programs are designed for children to use telescopes to study space. Other institutions that use scientific principles like power plants are beginning to design tours for older children. Older children can don hard hats and witness energy in action. All these examples serve to illustrate how the science museum of not so long ago is very different from what many visitors are likely to find today.

These new science museums are different from other museums in a number of important ways. First, science museums house experiments to be conducted in the present. Scientific principles identified centuries ago can be observed now. The history of the original moment of identification or the biography of the discoverer may accompany an exhibit, but the focus of the exhibit is on performing the experiment.

The opportunity to make predictions and see the results is another way that science museums differ from other types of museums. The *Predictor Me* is not able to see what it would be like to place a cabin by the shoreline in a landscape or change a color in an abstract painting. The ability of museum-goers to test a theory is totally unique to the science museum. Successful prediction is a way of testing what the museum-goer understands. The skills of predicting and estimating grow increasingly useful as children become more involved with the world in which they live. Science museum experiments challenge the *Predictor Me* to construct an arch that stands up or create the largest possible bubble. Because children are actually conducting experiments at the science museum, building block arches, or blowing a giant bubble, their actions demonstrate their powers of prediction. The "touchability" of science museum exhibits is a dizzying thought to many adults, a thought that beguiles some parents into considering the science museum as a playground or babysitter. Many children need assistance to operate the experiments or understand the underlying principle of an exhibit. As the subsequent discussion on *Balancing the Learning Equation* shows, the adult is a very important part of the science museum visit.

Science and Scientific Thinking

With art museums, it was shown how the recognition that art was a made thing helped clarify what exactly art is to the museum-goer. At science museums some visitors experience a similar confusion about what they perceive science to be as compared with the exhibits they see. The most common misconception about science is that it represents a body of facts. Nothing could be further from the truth. "Science is really a process," says Eddie Goldstein, Math and Science Education Specialist at the Capital Children's Museum. "Science is a method of looking at things—trying out ideas and seeing what happens." Scientific thinking is a life skill that encourages museum-goers to identify, classify, and understand the way a process works.

Scientific thinking caused a seven-year-old to announce one day that he was no longer afraid to be in his school bus during a thunderstorm. This boy was applying what he had learned about electricity from a demonstration in a science museum. During the program it had been clearly shown how vehicles shield the occupants by diverting the lightning. When the child understood the process himself, he was able to make the prediction that he would be safe on the bus in a thunderstorm. This is powerful information for a child because it enhances his understanding of his relationship in a changing world and increases his ability to work with the forces that operate in the world.

A Source of Science

The family museum-goer soon discovers that there is no place quite like a science museum. Because homes and schools have multifocused interests and demands, it is difficult to duplicate the resources available at the science museum. The science museum's exhibits are highly accessible and are dedicated to infusing science and technology with fun, action, and involvement.

Resources, expertise, and funds available to museums have an inherent advantage that cannot be duplicated at home or in school. The exhibits have been researched carefully and constructed for maximum durability and safety. With these exhibits available to everyone scientific learning is much easier than it would be if individual families attempted to create the exhibits at home.

The key to scientific learning is participation. Don Herbert, known to most television viewers as Mr. Wizard, said, "The reason I have kids on the show is that I know kids have more fun participating. I am interested in their having fun." For young children, fun is the tie that binds. The principles, the theories, and the facts all come later. A beginning in scientific study, which is based on doing, engages interest more soundly than a study based on memorizing facts from a page or viewing the contents of a glass case.

The staff of the science museum is another important source of scientific information. Informed lovers of science can be found throughout any science museum. They eagerly lend a hand when family museum-goers need additional information or help operating equipment. Because they offer the combination of their collections, laboratories, and informed sources, science museums present an exceptional opportunity for learning about the world.

Ways of Looking

As with all family museum visits, if engendering a love of museums is the goal, then the children are the ones who will determine much of what the family will see and do. This discussion considers the qualities of looking at science that transcend just seeing. The family can make their visit more enjoyable through an awareness of the challenges and potential of this way of looking.

The pace of a science visit affects how the family looks at the museum. Knowing when to slow down and when to walk on can be confusing. If a child is puzzling and continuing to ask questions about an exhibit, an adult can give enough time and patience to the child to continue his quest. It is not uncommon for children to struggle with an exhibit ten times without success until they figure it out. Encouraging this tenacity in a child is a great way for an adult to honor the *Inquisitive Me*. The dilemma for the adult is balancing the desire to keep the momentum going and recognizing a child's need to dawdle.

The elements of a science museum look include more than the eyes. The touching hand, the hearing ear, the smelling nose, and the tasting mouth are all ways to "look" at science. A good look at science requires the family to use as many senses as possible. When a child observes, "It's a green rock," his powers of looking have just begun. At the science museum he can take the green rock and touch it, scratch it, and look at it under a magnifying glass. It is this personal manipulation that results in discovery. Using multiple senses allows the museum-goer to classify and, therefore, organize his view of the world. An accurate observation of a rock or a star system requires using more senses than just sight. Encouraging children to use all their senses heightens their sensitivity and enriches the depth and breadth of their relationship with their world.

Multiple-sense experiences become deeply rooted in a child's memory preparing the *Remembering Me* for complex systems of thought. Anyone who has experienced a sudden flood of memories inspired by the smell of a certain food or the tune of an old song knows the intricate details the brain stores that can be ignited by the senses.

Regularly scheduled demonstrations of scientific principles or phenomena that inspire audience participation are an integral part of the activities offered in these museums. Eddie Goldstein believes that science museum demonstrations and other manipulative exhibits allow children . . . "to start making discoveries for themselves." When sci-

ence is found in this manner, according to Goldstein, the family can
. . . "see science not as a bunch of things to memorize but a way of
looking at the world, or dealing with the unknown."

At the Science Museum of Virginia, a young man was demonstrating electricity as part of the regularly scheduled programs. To demonstrate some of the effects of electricity, he chose children from the audience to participate on stage. One demonstration involved using a device that caused hair to stand up straight. Another device required a
person to stand inside a metal structure in a simulation of how lightning is grounded without harming the individual inside. The children
were at once spell-bound and filled with self-importance. They had
become part of science. Further demonstrations of lightning safety met
with a roomful of eager assistants.

The enthusiasm in the audience originated with the opportunity to
see scientific processes at work. Obviously, the entertaining aspect of
the demonstration added to the excitement the children and adults felt
toward the subject of electricity. Most people, however, recognized
that the demonstration had specific applications to their everyday lives.

When observing children at a science museum, Capital Children's Museum's Ed Lee, Physical and Biological Sciences Specialist, advises, "Watch their hands. Look at what they are changing and how they are changing it." The children's success or failure in figuring out an exhibit depends on their ability to follow directions. Many exhibits require reading instructions to make the experiment work; other exhibits ask children to listen to recorded messages or live demonstrators and follow their oral instructions. A child's hands offer visible evidence of how well they have understood directions.

Previous chapters have emphasized certain types of questions as a means of intriguing a child. These same questions are also helpful at the science museum. Questions are one of the best clues for finding out if a child is involved in thinking and wondering. An adult who is not a scientist may be uncomfortable not knowing the answer to many of these questions; however, what the adult does know is that answers can be provided by many resources at the museum. During the science visit, adults set a good example when they demonstrate how to find the answer to a question.

At the Exploratorium in San Francisco, a popular exhibit consisted of a dissection of animal eyeballs by an Explainer (a staff member). Although not for the squeamish, this type of live exhibit serves to demystify science in much the same way as living history events reveal human behavior.

The Armed Forces Medical Museum, one of the oldest museums in Washington, D.C., takes the demystification process further. This museum presents challenging ways of looking at the human body. Their exhibits feature healthy and diseased specimens of livers, lungs, hearts, fractured bones, and many other body parts. Children are fascinated to see these real human hearts and brains. Although some children may giggle or withdraw in horror, most children welcome the opportunity to look at the human body freely and objectively.

Balancing the Learning Equation: The Role of the Adult

The learning equation at the science museum is calculated by placing the total of a child's skills and knowledge plus the physical requirements of the exhibit on one side of the equation and placing the successful and enjoyable discovery of new insights on the other. Sometimes the child may signal for assistance from the family to supplement the skills and knowledge side of his equation. The decision of when to offer the child assistance is a personal one, but there are certain signals during a visit that can help adults identify the time to assist. If a child walks over to an exhibit, looks at it, and sits down to operate the controls, then he has found something that interests him and has made it work. In contrast, a child who lingers over an exhibit playing casually with the switches or persistently returning to the exhibit without actual participation is clearly signaling his interest and his inability to figure it out. A watchful adult can readily assist in balancing the learning equation by describing or restating what the exhibit is trying to accomplish. With that personal description, children are able to decide whether to go on with the exhibit or find a different one.

The clearest signal a child can give is to openly say, "I don't get this." Children recognize that adults have skills that make exhibits easier to manipulate or understand. What the following examples have in common is that an adult was needed at an early stage in the museum visit to stabilize the learning equation. Sometimes children need help in reading and sometimes in turning knobs and levers. At other times, exhibit explanations are simply confusing to a child.

When children experience problems getting involved with an exhibit that interests them, an adult can help them get started. By describing an exhibit's topic and how it works, the adult can remove the hurdle of reading difficulty that many exhibits present. For example, two six-year-old boys discovered the telegraph exhibit at the Science Museum of Virginia. They tapped at the keys, looked at the Morse code poster, tapped some more, and lingered—all clear invitations for the adult companion to become involved. Both boys evidently were unable to make the connection between what they saw on the poster and the tap-tap-tap of the switch.

The adult began to describe the exhibit: "Morse code is a way to send messages by sounds. What sound does the poster say stands for the letter A?" "Period, line," said the boys. "Right," the adult replied and then made one short sound and one long sound with the key. "Mr. Morse called them dots and dashes. The dot is a short sound and the dash is longer." "Oh, I get it," cried one of the boys and directed his friend to go to the other station so he could receive his message.

In this example, the adult was involved initially in offering a simple explanation of the exhibit, but the involvement did not include directing the children to take any action. After the boys decided what they wanted to do, the adult stayed to act as secretary and interpreter to insure the success of sending and receiving Morse code messages.

When a child masters an exhibit, adults need to recognize and applaud the event. In this case, the two boys sent message after message without any adult intervention. Knowing that repetition is fundamental to enjoyment, the adult affirmed each of their successes to build confidence in what they had accomplished. Once a child is successful with an exhibit, he naturally wants to do it again and again because he has felt the thrill of success.

Each time the child visits the museum, he masters more exhibits. When an adult can extend a child's success with a question or change of perspective, the child begins to add layer upon layer of meaning to experience. Just as with art and history, when the adult sees growth in the child's confidence he can begin to extend the knowledge with "What if" questions. These kinds of questions cause a child's understanding to grow if the adult is sensitive to the child's interests and abilities. To extend the child's looking at the telegraph, the adult asked,

"What if we used this telegraph instead of a telephone?" After sending a few messages, one boy responded, "It sure takes a long time just to say hello." "Right," the other boy agreed, "talking is a lot faster." Because these boys had actually used the telegraph over and over, their familiarity gave them latitude to hypothesize from first-hand experience, instead of guessing at how it might have been.

Science museum exhibits sometimes frustrate pudgy hands that are still working out how to do what the brain directs. Exhibit specialists constantly seek ways to create exhibits that are highly durable. One of the dilemmas for the science museum staff is damage to an exhibit caused by frustrated visitors. Some young visitors simply do not understand how the exhibit works or are physically unable to manipulate the controls. Adults need to stand ready to offer assistance, especially when valuable equipment is being misused. Keyboards can be rendered worthless by unattended five-year-olds who are unable to decipher an exhibit's purpose.

A child's frustration with an exhibit can be productive. Frustration shows children that some scientific investigation requires a degree of tenacity. Mastering a subject means there is a period of trial and error, trying, failing, trying again, and maybe failing again. When experiments do not go as planned, scientists do not give up. Instead, they observe what has happened, record the experiment, and come to an understanding. In dealing with young children, adults need to be ready to offer similar guidance in helping the child to achieve the desired level of enjoyment and understanding.

Nonproductive frustration can result in unintentional abuse of museum property where knobs are twisted off and terminals jammed because a child expected to be able to do something and could not succeed by himself. Both a child's age and his reading level are indicators of whether he or she possesses the necessary patience for scientific discovery. Generally, children in second grade and above have an *Adjustable Me* who can withstand several failures without becoming highly frustrated. Adults need to look for early signs of nonproductive frustration, such as hitting and banging, and be prepared to step in and offer help.

For the adult, balancing the learning equation is a matter of being with the child and being prepared to share the skills of reading, interpreting, and manipulating. The cautionary note is that many adults have the tendency to take over and complete the experiment for the child. Adults who take time to notice what the child is doing and who are willing to share their descriptive and monitoring abilities accompany children who leave the museum wanting to come back.

The Museum Is not School, The Adult Is not Teacher

Because of the numbers of children, schools cannot allow each child the luxury of finding his own way in science, art, or history. At worst learning in school deteriorates into a lock-step pattern of rote information and retrieval of fact. The museum is not school and there is no possibility of a failing grade. George Tressel of the National Science Foundation believes that the first step toward science enrichment at the science museum is for . . . "children to learn what is important to them."

Schools cannot always personalize scientific learning for children but parents can. Parents are valid observers of the quality of their children's enthusiasm. During museum visits, children whose interests are honored are spared the frustration of being unable to go where their natural interest takes them. Although teachers are denied much latitude in school because of the constraints of time and numbers of students, parents can take the time, be patient, and exercise the resourceful thinking necessary to make the museum visit rewarding for the child.

A parent knows when his child is having a good time or is under stress. When a seven-year-old runs around a roaring computerized dinosaur repeating, "You're weird, you're weird," with an intense little voice, the parent not only recognizes the child's excitement but also senses the fear the child is trying to mask. The parent's presence allows the child to work through those fears with someone he trusts and someone he does not have to share with 23 other children.

One Family's Visit

A family visit to the museum has many dynamics. Their expectations combined with the reality of the exhibits can present formidable problems. By following one family through six hours of science museum-going, readers can see how this family managed multiple age levels and a surprising complication.

One winter day a family with three children waited one hour in freezing weather to reach the lobby of the Maryland Science Center at 11:00 AM. They wished they had arrived earlier. (They had broken the cardinal rule of museum-going which recommends early arrival to avoid crowds.)

Featured at the center that day was an exhibit of large animated dinosaurs which growled and roared. When six-year-old Nathan, a long-time dinosaur enthusiast for whom the visit was planned, noticed the dinosaur growling in the foyer, he stiffened in terror and commenced crying and begging to go home.

While holding Nathan's stiff and trembling body, his mother realized that his father could take the two girls, ten-year-old Sarah and four-year-old Katie, to another exhibit. Holding Nathan, talking to him, and mocking the dinosaurs, his mother slowly walked Nathan to the center of the room. Nathan was still petrified. Nathan, who owned at least 200 diminutive toy dinosaurs and was able to growl with the finest tiger at the zoo, fell apart in front of mechanized monsters.

"But Nathan, I thought you liked dinosaurs," his mother said.

"I like them when they're little and they don't move," Nathan said firmly. "I like bones."

While they had been talking, the mother noticed that there was a Claymation movie which offered an option for them to explore. It was peace at last. Katie and Sarah had bonded and happily bounced off to play with dinosaur bones. Nathan followed his own interest to the energy room. Later at the cafeteria, the family found themselves ringside to the mechanical dissection of one of the dinosaurs, the one that had frightened Nathan so badly. After the family watched the wires and circuits of the dinosaur being repaired during lunch, Nathan's courage swelled.

After three hours in the museum it was time to go to a special movie for which they had tickets. When the movie was over, Nathan was ready to work through the dinosaurs, even *Tyrannosaurus rex*. Four hours after he had first uttered, "I want to go home," Nathan confronted the dinosaurs. He growled. He made fun of them. "Behave or I'll unplug you," he laughingly said. The visit continued for two more hours. Everyone left satisfied and smiling.

The reaction of Nathan's parents was very admirable. When presented with Nathan's condition, other parents might have retaliated with, "If you are going to act that way, we're taking you home and never taking you to another museum!" This threat can work with some children, but at what expense? This kind of discipline has questionable application at the museum.

With incidents like Nathan and the dinosaur, adults need to look for the cause. Are there too many expectations? Are the children feeling well? A few words from parents about public and private behavior have calmed many a storm. The most admirable quality of Nathan's family visit is that the parents had the needed patience.

Notice also in the story that there was much physical and verbal exchange among the family members. When Nathan erupted in the lobby, his mother took a physical reading on Nathan as well as what he was saying. Children send mixed signals. While Nathan's words were, "Let's go home," his body, although tense, was leaning toward the museum. He was not pulling on his mother to go away. He was not running from his father's side to the parked car. In this case, it was lucky that Nathan's mother could translate his words and actions.

Nathan's parents also knew him well. He was known as a dinosaur nut among his friends. Because of this interest, his mother and father wanted to help him overcome his fear. They wanted to help him by taking time, talking with him, and doing whatever was necessary. By being generously patient, allowing him to sidestep the intended exhibit and find an exhibit that offered safety, and then returning to the dinosaur much later in the day, the family could bring home a little boy who had some very important information to share with anyone who would listen. He came, he saw, he conquered.

Special Science Museum Considerations

The science museum is very adaptable to a family's needs. When energy levels are high, the action of the hands-on exhibits is very attractive to children and adults. Many science museums offer the choice of films and/or planetariums. The regularly scheduled films in their theaters offer some spectacular visual entertainment.

Some museums have installed special theatres with an IMAX projection system which features high-resolution images on five-story screens and high quality sound. Some movies carry a warning that the volume of sound can be frightening to children under three years of age. If the family consists of very young children, it would be advisable for one parent to be ready for a quick exit.

Science museums often design special rooms and programs for young children who need a cozier environment. Exhibits in these rooms do not require the same manipulative skills required by others. It is a good idea to request information and schedules a few days in

advance so that all the opportunities can be reviewed and both adults and children have some idea of what to expect.

Remember that visits to science museums are family experiences. Some adults may find that all they need to do is get their children in the museum and the museum does the rest. Other adults find they need to provide special ground rules for the older children or enlist the help of babysitters or extra adults so that each child has a chance to enjoy the museum to the fullest. All families benefit when the guideline of *not rushing* is followed. While rushing is discouraged at all museums, a child can find the science museum so exciting that he rushes through exhibits as if somehow the exhibits were going to disappear.

Post-Visit Activities

The science museum gift shop is a great resource for families who have enjoyed the museum. Books, models, kits, and toys provide the family with other sources of home-study science. In addition, the education department of the museum often offers special classes and workshops for children on all kinds of topics. Writing to the museums, calling for special events schedules, and asking to be put on their mailing lists are all ways to keep informed about science activities. Other sources of supplemental science education can be found at the library, bookstore, and special clubs.

At the conclusion of the science museum visit, the scientific way of looking at the world can come home to play. Similar to the gallery games suggested in Chapter Three, observation games can entertain children and exercise their scientific thinking. Look in the backyard. Notice the contrasts and similarities in the garden. The planning of a garden leads naturally to exploring environmental science. Where to dig? What effects do fertilizer and bone meal have on the soil?

Take science inside the house; explore the everyday world. Why do appliances and tools work a certain way? How does a faucet draw water? Is there a vacuum in the vacuum cleaner? Scientific thinking has led to many innovations and technological advances in the family's daily life. The science museum can nurture an interest in the how and why of these events. Science in the home and backyard furthers the same demystification process which began at the museum.

And the Deduction Is . . .

For every action there is a reaction. This statement is a basic law of the universe. Where science museums are concerned, every visit creates a reaction within the family. Science museums are places of inspiration, a habitat where new thoughts come to be, and more often than not, opportunities to experiment with fine equipment and benefit from the expertise of scientific professionals.

The science museum is like an older brother's chemistry set, a father's tool bench, and the hospital laboratory all rolled into one and waiting to be enjoyed. There are no tests. No assignment is due on Monday. The science museum visit needs to be "free" of all such restrictions. It is a public place of enjoyment and learning.

Knowledge of science makes the family less vulnerable to unfounded fears. The science museum can give a seven-year-old the power to understand electricity and ride his school bus in a thunderstorm without fear. A child who experiments, predicts, and discovers his influence on the physical world becomes familiar with the powers that are at work within that world. This knowledge of science allows a child to leave behind a powerless and fearful self and step forward to claim the power of knowledge as his own.

Chapter Seven
Children's Museums: Children in Charge

"May the force be with you."

—Obi-Wan Kenobi *Star Wars*

T he force that fuels the adventure through childhood is not to be found under a microscope or even on a report card; it is not something that can be measured by scales or saved by refrigeration. The force within a child is evident in his own innate curiosity. At school and at home, a child's curiosity is cultivated by listening and reading; yet, it is through the child's play, his doing, that his curiosity is made into something he can recognize.

In the previous chapters, the museum visit often succeeded when the children were given the power to follow their *Curious Me*. Nowhere is this principle more important than with a new breed of museums known as children's museums and discovery rooms. These alternative museums place children in charge. Yet, like all the other types of museums discussed in this book, the child still needs, "An adult who cares what a child thinks, will listen to their questions, and not rush," according to Barbara Waters of the Cape Cod Natural History Museum.

In contrast to halls lined with glass cases and untouchable art, these alternative museums immediately encourage children to learn by doing. These museums are science museums for the younger child. Although many of these facilities retain the name "museum," they are not traditional museums in that they do not save things and do not place a high requirement on reading skills. Instead, administrators of children's museums are more interested in preserving something more precious than any artifact, that is, the *Confident Me* who wants to learn independently.

These museums are popular with adults and children because they fulfill several needs. First, families are drawn to them not just for their entertainment value, but for the opportunity for children and parents to do something together. Second, the children's museum is viewed as a safe area. There are no paintings to worry about touching, and all exhibits are meant to be walked through, sat in, or manipulated. Within minutes of entering, museum-goers find that it has not only been child-proofed but also parent-proofed. To a large extent this liberates the family. A safe environment relieves a child (and his adult companion) from numerous concerns about a child's behavior in a public place, and it frees the parent and child from traditional roles of parent/guide, child/follower. Finally, these children's museums supplement the school curriculum. Budget cuts have reduced science and art programs so much that many parents look at these centers as resources to fill in the holes of a child's (and secretly, an adult's) education.

Ways of Looking

There are three ways of looking that influence the family's experience at the children's museums: the learning-by-doing approach, the opportunity to choose, and the control of the visit. Each of these ways of looking underlines why children's museums are so different from school, other traditional museums, or even home. One seven-year-old seasoned museum-goer summed up why he enjoyed children's museums so much: "I like the children's museum because they don't try to tell you stuff."

Learning-By-Doing

Children's museums serve as introductions to other kinds of museums. The *Touching Me, Exploring Me,* and *Pretending Me* are all welcomed at the children's museum. While learning occurs at a children's museum, as it does in all museums, the learning is less self-conscious. Here, the *Learning Me* wears a *Playing Me* disguise. The idea of learning by doing involves many simple and complex acts of play.

A child who learns by doing is actually combining a minimum of two senses. Sometimes these multiple senses receive conflicting messages, such as the radish that looks good but tastes bad, or the object that looks light but feels heavy. Whatever is felt, smelled, or tasted is experienced in a completely personal way. Like the science museum, the children's museum encourages the use of many senses in various combinations as an exciting and unique type of learning.

Understanding this concept is critical to realizing why children's museums are so loved by children. At many schools there is some learning-by-doing but always under the watchful eye of the teacher. Also, there can be a real fear of failure. What if the child is unable to do the thing right? At children's museums most exhibits are designed so that children do not fail. At the Richmond Children's Museum's "Playworks" exhibit, a child can pretend to be a banker, a teller, or a customer using realistic bank forms and paper money. They try on all the adult world they want without any of the pressures. No one is given instructions on how to fill out bank receipts or how to keep the balance in the checkbook. The child takes cues from the setting and makes decisions about what he can and cannot do. The importance is placed on encountering the formalities of banking without the consequences of miscalculation.

The touchability factor in learning by doing is important developmentally, not only for the child's sense of enjoyment, but also for more complex and subtle brain development. The way that children approach more complicated ideas, theories, or systems in their lives is based on early experiences of manipulating objects on their own. "Children who have not acquired a feel for the laws of the lever through playing with seesaws will have difficulties in acquiring such an understanding in their high school physics class. Children who have not played with beads, rods, and lumps of clay may have difficulties in understanding addition, subtraction, multiplication, and division."[1]

At a children's museum there may not be as much evidence of quantifiable learning as parents like. A child may not be finding out where Abe Lincoln got shot or other important facts, but the child's learning is disguised by all the fun the he is having.

On the other hand, what exactly is a five-year-old learning as she squeals with delight pretending to drive a bus at a children's museum? Is she role-playing in her fantasy? Is she finding how important she feels or how big the steering wheel is? It may be that children extract meaning in a completely different way from the way adults imagine

---

[1] N.L. Gage and D.C. Berliner, *Educational Psychology*, Houghton Mifflin, Boston. 1979. page 56.

they do. The little five-year-old may have just learned that she and her two friends, and sometimes her little brother, can fit exactly on the bus seat. She is also learning how to become comfortable in a public setting. The *Experimentor Me* is encouraged to be at work in a public institution. The *Doing Me*, interacting in a physical and mental way, broadens a child's ability to think in detail.

The advantage of this method of learning is that it is extremely humanizing. For example, how extraordinary it is for a child to realize that a 19th-century child (probably about his own size) had to turn the cream separator just like this one about 200 turns before he was finished with his chores! Once today's child has tried it for a few minutes, he realizes how sore the arm must have become. At Rose Hill Manor Children's Museum, children have the opportunity to experience the 1800s by working on a quilt, combing wool, and playing with typical toys of the period. When a child can touch historical artifacts, products of nature, or technological wonders, history is no longer something someone else made, grew, or invented. He now has tangible information as to how it might have felt for a child his size and age to live during another time.

The Opportunity to Choose

Another characteristic of children's museums that differentiates them from other institutions is the opportunity they provide for the child to make choices. The ability to make choices, safe choices and unedited choices, is extremely important to the child. Almost intuitively a child knows that any choice is acceptable at the children's museum because there are no dangerous choices offered. Seldom in a child's world is the choice of what to do and where to go so completely left up to him.

The following example illustrates how much a child delights in the act of choosing (not necessarily the choice itself). Two mothers and their four children (ages 6 to 8) recently visited the Capital Children's Museum. In the lobby the mothers discovered a computer for the children to plan their itinerary at the museum. A program prompted the children to enter their names and ages and then asked them to choose three exhibits to visit. The four children took immediate delight in the process. The mothers were enlisted to help read some of the choices and assist in typing their names. After 25 minutes in the lobby, each child had his own itinerary and map in hand. The mothers were anxious to get started, but the children were enjoying themselves immensely. They had been given the power to choose and they loved it. They did not care that they were still in the lobby or that the entire museum awaited them; it was their time and their choice. Several times during that 25 minutes the mothers considered breaking off the computer task. But because both mothers agreed they did not want to interfere while the children were engaged, they let the computer itinerary exercise continue.

Control of the Visit

The final characteristic of a visit to the children's museum is control. Children need to feel they are in control to enjoy a visit to a children's museum thoroughly. This is one place where a child can spend as much time as he wants on the exhibit of his choice, a place where an eight-year-old girl can be endlessly interested in tortilla-making or completely uninterested in computers. This is the one place where the *Museum-Goer's Bill of Rights and Responsibilities* is tested minute by minute.

Let the story of the two mothers and four children in the lobby of the Capital Children's Museum explain the difference between giving children control and giving them choices. The company had made their way up to the second floor. Without consulting their maps or their mothers, the children found a child-sized maze to crawl around and get lost in. After examining the four itineraries, it was discovered that no one had selected the maze. The mothers asked the children if they were concerned that the maze was not an item they had selected to visit. A resounding chorus of, "No," echoed down the hall. The children had spent time choosing, abandoned their original idea for the interest of the moment, and retained control of the day when they charged full throttle into the maze.

Within the maze the children had control of their time. They walked and ran through it. They played hide and seek in it. They played tag. They found at least five positions from which to say, "Hi, Mom." The mothers would occasionally ask if the children were ready to go, but they set no limits. The truth is that children would have been content if the visit stopped right there. They had chosen this delightful activity and were thrilled to be given the chance to remain there as long as they wanted. One mother commented to the other, "They act like they have all the time in the world." (At this point, an hour had passed and the six of them had only been to the lobby and one exhibit.)

This example illustrates how different a visit is when the child is truly in control. As soon as parents say, "I think it's time to go on," or "Let's go see Mexico," they have taken back control of the visit. Instead of asking these power-asserting questions, parents need simply ask, "Are you ready to go?" This allows the child the choice of moving on without weighing down his decision with adult values.

There is also a difference between letting a child make choices and letting a child misbehave. Children under four years do need some supervision. It is obviously unacceptable for Johnny to hit a strange three-year-old over the head with a fireman's boot from a dress-up corner. Likewise, it is unacceptable to let a child monopolize an exhibit when several other children are obviously waiting their turn. Adults who ask questions that inquire after their child's comfort and who participate if necessary, are in no way asserting control over the children and their visit; they are simply being responsible.

The Role of Repetition

Nursery school teachers recognize the power of repetition with pre-school children. Once a child is familiar with a routine, breaking the routine can seriously damage continuity. It is the same with children's museums. The exhibits do not change; in fact, it seems they will never change. Children find comfort in that fact and count on things being the same.

For young children the joy of repetition is rooted in performing the task; that is, doing the task over and over and over again, not necessarily knowing how to do it. On the second floor of the Capital Children's Museum in an exhibit named "The Cave," children walk down a dark hallway with the sound of dripping water helping to create a spooky atmosphere. Once the child understands that it is safe, he will return again and again to experience that feeling. Children's voices are often heard in the hallway: "Yes, it is scary," one little girl admits. "Why is it so dark?" a five-year-old worries. "Let's go out and walk in again," shout both children when they emerge from the cave.

Repetition also signals that the child is interested in an object. In a room of simple machines at the Capital Children's Museum, one exhibit explores the function of devices such as the lever and the pulley. Through experimenting with three types of pulleys, children discover that the cinder block with the most pulleys at the top is the easiest to lift. Children will pull the ropes again and again seemingly just to hear the crash of the block when it falls. They do not need someone to tell them why one is easier than the next; they need to do it over and over until they know it inherently.

Exhibits at Children's Museums

Earlier it was mentioned that families enjoy children's museums for their entertainment, for the child-proofing and parent-proofing qualities evident in the exhibits, and for the freedom from traditional parent/child roles. Exhibits at a children's museum offer a variety of choices from recreated historical rooms to occupational playtime roles such as bankers, grocers, or farmers, as well as activities that build on manipulative skills. Rose Hill Manor and the Cloister's Children's Museum in Baltimore, Maryland, offer exhibits where tools or toys from another time in history can be touched. Whatever the topic of the exhibit, the tools and toys are set up to allow children to play successfully with or without adult supervision.

Generally, people who design exhibits at children's museums are looking for durability as well as maximum playability. In contrast, traditional museums are often looking for ways to display and engage young minds without actually inviting them to use the exhibit. The high-touch exhibits at a children's museum allow the young children the chance to do some hands-on thinking during a time when their brains rely heavily on sensory stimulation.

From the Adult's Perspective

Many adults make the assumption that children's museums are designed just for children, but the new trend toward the hands-on museums consciously keeps the word children out of the title. The staff of the Hands-On Museum in Ann Arbor, Michigan, believes that leaving the word children out of the museum title enables adults and older children to feel comfortable and enjoy themselves there. It does work; adult singles as well as families return again and again to the museum.

The dilemma for parents is: Do they participate in the playing or let the child enjoy this time alone? What usually happens depends on their prior experiences with the child. If parents are known as a resource, then they will fall into the role of giving information and conducting the visit. Parents who are seen by their children as cohorts will be invited to join in the discovery. Parents need to realize that their history of involvement or noninvolvement in their children's activities influences what the child expects and how he behaves during the visit.

The role of the parent as advocate is as applicable to a children's museum as it is to a traditional museum. One early summer day, two mothers and their four children visited Rose Hill Manor Children's Museum. Here, both traditional museum concepts and hands-on history philosophies are combined. The museum is a historic home and, within its buildings and grounds, displays authentic artifacts of life during another century.

During one of the particular tours led by a docent, the two older children, an eight-year-old and a seven-year-old, appeared ready to visit the kitchen with the rest of the tour. However, the two younger children, aged five and six, had become so absorbed in working on a quilt that they did not want to go. Happily, one mother reassured the docent that she would watch the boys carefully and they would catch up with the tour in a few minutes. In this way, she honored the younger children's interest. The parent acted as advocate underlining their decision to choose to stay. In only a few minutes they were ready to approach the next stop on the tour with confidence and comprehension.

When taking tours with children, parents need to watch for signs of interest and be on the alert for the unusual event or question. When the tour of Rose Hill Manor concluded in the trolley and carriage barn, one mother noticed smoke coming from the blacksmith's shop. Although the tour had already been there, the two mothers and their children decided to investigate. They found a new blacksmith firing up the forge and checking out the equipment. For nearly an hour the four children were allowed to help fan the fire and watch the blacksmith hammer and pound to make a few simple hooks and nails. The room got smoky. Everyone's eyes were red and, in that brief time, the children realized how dirty one could get. Fanning the forge, a novelty at the beginning, was now work. Everyone had begun to see what this kind of job was really like. This chance opportunity stole the show. Acting as advocates and honoring the interest of their children, the parents were able to take advantage of what was there.

Some people might consider the above seemingly fortuitous occasion just lucky. In reality, luck had little to do with their good fortune. The mother was sensitive to what was going on around her and willing to ask for a special opportunity for the children. Other opportunities to chance upon interesting activities or stories often rest with the docent who is leading a tour. When adults engage the docent by asking for stories about children who once lived in the house, unexplained mysteries, or favorite artifacts, the child's understanding of a tour's potential is broadened. No longer does the *Curious Me* have to wait until the tour is over to have some fun.

During the school year the time of day chosen for a visit can influence its success. School tours often arrive in the morning and flood the children's museums through noon. Many museums advise families to visit in the afternoon when it is less crowded; however, families with youngsters who need naps must brave the morning hours. Sunday morning is less crowded than Saturday, and, finally, remember that museums are also crowded during bad weather. If time is limited at a children's museum, state the facts clearly beforehand. If all parties agree, assign time limits to itineraries. If children choose not to follow time limits, be sure they know the consequences. It might be helpful for the adult to say something such as, "I can't imagine how we are going to be able to see all the things here." Equipped with this knowledge, the child does not despair when it is announced it is time to go and he has only seen one floor.

Charge of the Little Brigade

A children's museum is a museum where children are in charge. The popularity of these museums results from their ability to provide the family with a comfortable, familiar, and enjoyable setting where they can pursue their *Playing Me* and *Do-It-Myself Me*. Visiting these museums, however, and taking full advantage of what they offer requires the same care and attention to a child's interest as traditional museums. Children's museums are designed for children to make choices and decide when they have had enough of an activity or exhibit. Adults are liberated from guessing when to go on and can enjoy the emerging independence of a child in charge in a place that was built for him!

Far from the adult world of orderliness and lists of restrictions, a place where a child can be in charge is a true refuge, an island in the sea

of powerlessness. When a child's ability to choose, be in control, and be curious is endorsed, a child's self-confidence takes a giant leap forward. When children are allowed to be in charge, their playing, their acting out, and their doing, become very powerful. At the children's museum, the child and adult have the opportunity to embrace playing as a way to learn together. Let the true force of their curiosity be known and there is no world they cannot conquer.

The Passing of the Keys

One day soon our children will begin the long-awaited journey into their future. Until that time we stand as gatekeepers to the present and the past. All the generations who have come before us have built a treasure house of knowledge—full of their work, their beliefs, and their creations. The keys they have used to unlock the mysteries and wonders of the world are in our keeping. They have been passed down from generation to generation.

Let us behold museums as places that celebrate the passing of these keys. Let us journey there as companions who value the treasures inside the museum and willingly share the keys. Then, let the world our children are about to inherit open and be theirs.

Appendix

The Art of Finding a Museum

Where's the Me *in Museum* can help the family find an infinite variety of *Me*'s at the museum. What is left to the adults in the family is actual finding the museum itself. To many families the museum is someplace they already know. For others, the following resources can help locate museums in a particular your field of interest or within a specific geographic region.

There are several basic reference books that can be consulted to discover more about certain museums. The most complete is the American Association of Museums' directory of over 65,000 museums which is organized by geographic region. Each entry contains basic information about a museum's collection and hours of operation. Recently published travel guidebooks offer specific information about the hours of operation, fees, parking, directions to the museum, and special services such as handicapped facilities and rentals of strollers. These books also highlight a museum's permanent collection. Many museums, especially art museums, change the work or objects on display, therefore it is a good idea to call ahead and confirm that a favorite object or work of art is still on exhibit. The fees at most museums are usually reduced for children, and some museum have instituted a maximum family (group) fee to encourage the entire family to visit and minimize damage to the pocketbook. In this vein many museums have regularly scheduled "free" days or evenings when all fees are waived.

Regional newspapers and magazines often include listings of rotating exhibits and special events. These exhibits might feature a certain artist, a type of airplane, or a newly excavated treasure. When returning to a previously visited museum, these "new" choices offer the family additional incentives to plan another visit. In addition, traveling exhibits like the spectacular King Tut exhibit offer a once-in-a-lifetime chance to view many incredible works of art or treasure.

Art, natural history, and science magazines feature articles on newly-installed exhibits or topics that relate to traveling exhibits. These periodicals also have selected listings that can be consulted to see what is happening in a particular field of interest. Travel magazines feature articles on visiting places with children and often include helpful logistical hints about where to stay, eat, and how to get there.

If the family is planning to visit a new destination, travel agencies can offer a great deal of information. They may have brochures on interesting sites and knowledge of when is the best time to visit. Pre-packaged tours are an easy way to give the family a general idea of where they are, but be sure tour schedules are flexible enough to allow for a child's physical needs. When planning a trip, children enjoy writing the Chamber of Commerce and Tourist Board for a schedule of upcoming events and interesting sites to visit. To improve chances of a quick response, try including in your child's letter of inquiry a stamped self-addressed envelope.

The concierge or front office at your hotel usually keeps an up-to-date file on what is going on in the area. They also have a number of free publications that are available upon request, as well as public transportation schedules and taxi fares to nearby museums.

Many museums keep neighboring libraries and community centers abreast of new programs. Look for announcements of special classes, reading lists, and workshops about topics related to museum exhibits on library or community bulletin boards.

Tips on Staying in Touch

A good way to find out about special exhibits and events at museums is to consider membership in the museum. For an annual donation most museums offer discounts in their shops, reduced entrance fees, informative newsletters, and schedules of special events.

When the family has a favorite site for which membership is not available, ask to be put on their mailing list. Many large sites such as Colonial Williamsburg Virginia have monthly newsletters that alert readers of upcoming events. If reservations are required for holiday candlelit walks or special children's activities, then the earlier one knows about it the better chance one has of obtaining tickets.

Selected Bibliography

The books listed below are excellent resources for the family. Many of them can be found at the library, local bookstores, or museum shops. While this selection is by no means complete, these titles can start the family on their way to discovering more about topics that relate to museums. Other suggestions can be obtained by writing the museum's education department.

Arms & Armour. Eyewitness Book Series. By Michele Byam. Knopf. 1988. Beautifully illustrated history of arms and armor from prehistoric weapons to guns that won the West.

Bet You Can't. By Vicki Cobb and Kathy Darling. Avon. 1980. Dozens of experiments using household items and demonstrating scientific principles. Recommended for grade seven and above but younger children also find it interesting.

The Book of Where or How to Be Naturally Geographic. By Neill Bell. Little, Brown and Company. 1982. Explores geography and map-making with dozens of activities.

Drawing with Children. By Mona Brookes. Jeremy P. Tarcher, Inc. 1987. Clear, sensible guide to drawing successfully. For parents and teachers.

Castles—A Guide for Young People. Published by HMSO. 1981. Small detailed illustrations and easy text. Describes castle-life room by room.

Everything Is Somewhere, The Geography Quiz Book. By Jack McClintock and David Helgren. Quill Morrow Publications. 1986. Games and activities for the whole family.

Great Painters. By Piero Ventura. G.P. Putnam & Sons. New York. 1984. Whimsical illustrations accompany reproductions that enlighten readers as to the surrounding culture of the artist.

How Things Work. Simon and Schuster. 1984. Clear and simple descriptions with full color illustrations about the scientific principles behind everyday appliances and other machines.

How Why When Where. By Belinda Hollyer, Jennifer Justice, John Paton. Arco Publishing Inc. 1984. Illustrated explanations of everything from turkeys to airplanes.

How Your Body Works, A Trip Around the Body Machine. By Judy Hindley and Christopher Rawson. Usborne Hayes Publisher. 1975. Comic strip like drawings and humorous text about body systems.

The Human Body. By Jonathan Miller and David Pellham. Viking 1983. A three-dimensional, accurate, movable illustrated book on the human body.

Just Look . . . A Book About Paintings. By Robert Cumming. Cameron & Tayleur Ltd. 1979. Excellent resource for elements of art. Beautiful reproductions with insightful questions that penetrate the artist's intentions and choices.

The Know How Book of Experiments. By Heather Amery. Usborne Hayes Publisher. 1977. Well-illustrated experiments for all ages.

Let's Get Lost in a Painting. Series of books by Ernest Goldstein. *The Gulf Stream*, (Winslow Homer); *The Peaceable Kingdom*, (Edward Hicks) *Washington Crossing the Delaware*, (Emmanuel Leutze); *American Gothic* (Grant Wood); and *The Brooklyn Bridge*, (Frank Stella). Garrard Publishing Company. 1982. Examine the choices that faced the artist and how the problems were solved. Revealing to adults and children.

Let's Go to the Art Museum. By Virginia K. Levy. Veejay Publications 1983. Basic introduction to the elements of art.

Looking at Art Series. Faces. By Giles Waterfield; *People at Home* and *People at Work*. By Patrick Conner. Atheneum. 1982. Examine in detail how art tells the human story.

Mommy, It's a Renoir! By Aline Wolf. Parent Child Press. 1984. An appreciation for children that uses postcards to identify master painters.

Science Activity Book. Smithsonian Family Learning Project. Galison Books. 1987. Twenty exciting experiments.

Science Fare, Illustrated Guide and Catalog of Toys, Books, and Activities for Kids. By Wendy Saul with Alan R. Newman. Harper & Row. 1986 Wonderful overall resource.

There Once Was a Time. By Piero Ventura. Putnam. 1986. Depicts historical events through the people, clothing, tools, shelter, and food of the period.